FRESHMAN AT FIFTY
A STORY OF DREAMS, DETERMINATION AND SELF-DISCOVERY

CARLA JOHNSTON

Johnston, Carla. *Freshman at Fifty: A Story of Dreams, Determination and Self-Discovery*

Copyright © 2021 by Carla Johnston

Published by KWE Publishing: www.kwepub.com

ISBN: Paperback 978-1-950306-71-8, Ebook 978-1-950306-72-5

Library of Congress Catalog Number: 2021915819

First Edition. All rights reserved. No part of this publication may be reproduced in any means, electronic or mechanical, including recording, photocopying, or any information storage or retrieval system, without the written permission of the author. The exception would be in the case of brief quotations embodied in the critical articles or reviews, and pages where permission is specifically granted by the authors. Although every precaution has been taken to verify the accuracy of the information contained herein, the authors assume no responsibility for any errors or omissions. The authors shall have neither liability nor responsibility to any person or entity with respect to loss or damage caused, or alleged to have been caused, directly or indirectly, by the information contained in this book.

To my son, Jim.

REVIEWS FOR FRESHMAN AT FIFTY

"From childhood through her teen years, Dr. Carla Johnston had to work harder than most can even imagine, attempting to avoid her father's wrath. Rarely allowed to spend time with friends, Dr. Johnston was forced to leave high school early each day to help keep her father's office afloat instead of taking the science classes that would have furthered her lifelong dream of becoming a doctor. As a young mother, Dr. Johnston had to again put her aspirations on hold, this time to support herself and her son. Throughout a string of marriages to men who seemed terrific until she dared verbalize her desire to attend college, Dr. Johnston tried desperately to give her son the family life and herself the support she never had. Working day and night, her eye also remained on the prize of becoming a doctor.

Freshman at Fifty takes the reader on the rollercoaster ride that was Dr. Carla Johnston's life, complete with twists, turns, and spirals. Buckle up and hang on tightly! Despite our life-long friendship, I found myself mesmerized while reading Dr. Carla Johnston's surreal true story, fraught with immeasurable heartache and unfettered determination. Get ready for the surprise ending!"
—Mary DeGrezia, PhD, RN

"The wondrous journey Dr. Johnston takes us on is a quest of the inner self, and the pursuit of self in all its colors of evolution. We, the audience, are taken on a deep dive into fears, doubts, insecurities, feelings of being unloved, the courage of will power and ultimately the self-love needed when our inner self is restless due to its desire to fulfill our soul's purpose, dreams and assignments while here on earth. *Freshman at Fifty* is a candid reminder of the obstacles we have faced and those yet to come. Dr. Johnson shares how in following our inner self, we are led to the freedom we yearn for, realization, fulfilled dreams, purpose that give true meaning and a silver lining of joy and contentment in our lives."
—Eva Garrick, M.Msc.

"As I read through each chapter, I could see and feel how the layering of Carla's life events created deep wounds that then turned into valuable Soul Lessons. In the end her strength and tenacity heals and opens you up to her self-realization of the beauty and perfection that lies within us. I appreciate Carla's courage in putting it all out there. I'm sure many will find themselves in this story!"
—Tracy Houchins, Advanced Soul Coach, Reiki Master Teacher, www.magicinthemess.com

CONTENTS

Foreword ix
Introduction xi

1. First Day 1
2. Square Peg in a Round World 5
3. College Dreams on Hold 13
4. Tenacious Pursuit of a Family 19
5. College Goals Revisited 29
6. My New Best Friend 39
7. A Dream Realized 45
8. My Life's Purpose 53
9. The Influence of Traditional Medicine 61
10. December 28th 69
11. Acting as If I Know What I Am Doing 75
12. Coloring Outside the Lines 87
13. My Journey Toward Life's Purpose 93
14. Calling for a Doctor 103
15. Graduation and A Final Goodbye 113
16. Life's Lessons Learned 123

About the Author 127

FOREWORD

As a Conversation Coach guiding clients to more clear and concise conversations, I am familiar with people who stick with a plan as long as there is no opposition. As long as they remain in the flow, all is well, but when experience changes to the ebbs it's a different story and maybe a change of directions. I have been working with clients for more than 20 years helping them figure out what speaks to their soul and how to bring it into their experience of life.

When Carla Johnston asked me to write the foreword for her book, her baby, I was honored. We've known each other for many years, through different industries. We have a beautiful way of reconnecting without effort every few years to remain in touch. Through the years of knowing Carla, she has been focused on learning. She is what we call a lifelong learner. She decided at an incredibly early age she wanted to be a doctor and despite many obstacles, she persevered. I love her focus and determination.

Freshman at Fifty is inspiring and motivating. Being a freshman at fifty takes courage and Carla shares her courage. This book explains how important it is to stay focused on your goals and never take your eyes off the prize. One of the things I like most is the vulnerability with which it is written. It talks about life. It shows how life happens all around us. It shows best how we go with the ebbs and flow of life.

This book helps you to understand and accept the changes of life because it is a personal story of perseverance and triumph. Carla is sharing her story about all the obstacles thrown at her, all the obstacles to dissuade her of the importance of her goals and her choices. There were times when she, like most of us, bent to the will of a different story only to always come back to herself and her goals. This is an amazing roadmap of focus, determination, perseverance, and the importance of saying YES to you.

It is my absolute pleasure to give you a glimpse of what is to come in the next few pages and a glimpse of Dr Carla Johnston courageously sharing her story. Enjoy.

Say yes to life!

Claudette W. Gadsden, The Conversation Coach
www.coachclaudette.com

INTRODUCTION

There are a few reasons that propelled me to take the leap and write this book. Over the years, I would hear someone comment on how lucky I was to achieve my goals consistently. Depending upon the circumstances, I might share details of my story, precisely the many obstacles I encountered along the way. They often expressed surprise, wanting to learn more about how I was able to stay focused and continue to move forward. This got me thinking about how we do not usually have the opportunity to see the "behind the scenes" work required when pursuing goals. Crossing the finish line of a race or walking across the stage at commencement are certainly celebratory moments. Such moments are most certainly the result of plenty of hard work and dedication. "Luck" takes plenty of grit, preparation, and tenacity- at least it has in my life.

Initially, I was hesitant to commit to putting my life on paper, fearing judgment and ridicule. My first draft was a fictional story, obscuring the names of places and changing the names of everyone mentioned in the book. My son, Jim, pushed me to consider changing my plan—to write a nonfiction book. He felt that it was necessary to tell my story, warts and all. Through the incredible support of my son, I began writing my story—using his name and mine. His strength and encouragement permitted me to be brave, take a chance, and be vulnerable. With that said, everyone else mentioned in this book has had their names changed. To my mind, it does not take away from my experiences and ensures their privacy.

It is a massive leap of faith to document my missteps and mistakes. Ironically, through this process, I find myself less judgmental of others, having empathy for those who find themselves in similar circumstances. Yes, we all make mistakes—at least what we consider to be mistakes at the moment. Time and time again, especially in my case, these missteps led me to incredible learning and self-discovery.

With gratitude, I acknowledge a few people who have played a significant role in my life.

I was introduced to Judith Roark over twenty years ago, and we began working together. She continues to be my counselor, confidant, and life coach to this day. Judith is incredibly gifted, insightful, and supportive. Her guidance has allowed me to shed my shame, guilt, and self-doubt while creating space for dreams and designing a life that brings me joy, creativity, and purpose. It is impossible to imagine my life without her listening ear, expertise in shifting internal dialogue, constant guidance, and support. She nurtured my dreams right alongside me, pushing when I stalled and encouraged when I needed a moment to breathe.

Working with my business coach, Claudette Gadsden, I mentioned my goal of writing a book based on my life experiences. She and I created a plan, one that required me to make an effort to move this desire forward. Claudette gave me the name of a local self-publishing firm, KWE Publishing, and said it was up to me to make the connection; make that first move. She was spot-on; it was what I needed to hear to shift from fear to action. Claudette's brilliant guidance and support allowed me the ability to visualize and create a successful plan for this goal. Her recommendation resulted in my introduction to Kim Eley, my editor and publisher. Kim has been one of my biggest cheerleaders, encouraging me when fear and doubts stalled forward progress. Her infectious laughter and kind demeanor created an atmosphere of collaboration that ultimately allowed me the room to blossom as a writer.

In addition to my sisters, there have been so many friends and colleagues who have graciously pushed me to move forward with this book. I am eternally grateful to all of them! They have enthusiastically supported me during this process, encouraging me to be brave and strong. All of them have, and continue, to inspire me- challenging me to *'Live out Loud.'*

This book is my endeavor at *Living Out Loud*!

FIRST DAY

Taking a deep breath, I stop momentarily at the entrance. Confidently, I open the heavy door. A loud squeaking sound is quickly followed by a booming, bellowing echo that results in a final thud. Inside, I mentally reassure myself that everything will be fine; I will quietly and quickly enter the classroom, grabbing a seat in the back without bringing any attention to myself. I smile nervously as I make my way down the hallway. Once through the narrow entranceway, I stop. I am stunned. It is not a classroom at all. I am entering a theatre-style lecture hall that looks as if it could accommodate about 500 students. My knees begin to shake as I realize that I am standing in the front of the lecture hall, ground-floor level, directly in front of the professor's desk! My grand entrance, for everyone to see! I stop breathing. So much for my quiet, unassuming entrance.

Good going, Carla, good going. My mind is barking, *just keep going and find a seat as quickly as you can.* So up the nearest ramp I go, heading toward the hall's back entrance, which leads directly to the seats now being claimed by others. I will remember this next time. The back of the room is filling up quickly, and I am relieved to see an empty row just ahead.

I grab my seat, taking out my notebook. My hands are sweating; my heart is pounding as I begin to calm my nerves. *Whew! So far, so good.* I am here on time and ready to go. I slowly start looking around the room, smiling to myself. I am amused to see that so many of these young people look like they just rolled out of bed; some even appear to be still wearing what they had on while they were *in* bed! Silently I think, y*es, you blend in well and fit right in; dressed in a business suit.* Pajamas aren't an option for me. As soon as this class wraps, I have to head to work.

The crowd is moving in, filling up the seats around me, but not next to me. My entire row is empty, leaving a noticeable gap. An observer would think that I have some sort of contagious condition requiring isolation. Minutes before class begins, the late arrivals have no choice but to sit in my row, and it quickly fills up.

Thinking, *"Well, here I go,"* finally beginning my journey to attend my first day at the University of Maryland, Baltimore County. My mood perfectly matches this warm sunny morning. Beautiful white trees line the street, inviting me onto the campus. I have been preparing for this moment for such a long time! Despite so many setbacks and challenges, I am finally here!

This morning, I felt just like a kid, packing my bookbag with all my new supplies and a copy of my class schedule along with a campus map. Being organized is always a priority. I took a final look in the mirror before leaving. My reflection confirmed that I wasn't a young woman heading to college just after high school. I am an older returning student. I know that I will be attending classes with students who are the same age as my son. That was obvious when I visited the campus to meet with my academic advisor. I noticed that she used the term "non-traditional" student. Non-traditional is undoubtedly a term that fits most of my life. No matter the label, I am just so excited to be here.

My heart races as I drive onto campus with a shiny, new parking pass dangling from my mirror. I quickly find a parking spot. I am thirty minutes early, and I am taking no chances; I do not want to be late. I review my map once again, making sure I am in the correct parking lot. I do not want to get a ticket on my first day! I soak up the sunshine and the birdsongs as I head toward Lecture Hall One. I have a good idea where I am going. Or so I think.

The campus is crowded with young people chatting and walking along the pathways between the tall buildings. Strangely, I see Lecture Halls Two and Three, but I can't spot my building. *How can I miss a lecture hall?* I retrace my steps up and down the pathway, re-reading the signs as I begin to panic silently. *Where the heck is it? I don't want to be late!* I muster the courage to ask a passerby, a young man who graciously points to a building down the hill, informing me that the entrance is on the backside of the building. "Don't worry, a lot of people miss it the first time," he says with a smile. *Okay, back on track.*

At the start of the hour, right on cue, the professor enters the room. He immediately outlines his expectations for the class. It is my first chemistry class in decades, so I am concentrating on every word. Moving to the board, he writes an incredibly complex equation and asks for the solution. I smile to myself, thinking he's joking, trying to get our attention, seeing if we're engaged. Surely the equation is an example of what we will be learning in this class. To my surprise, everyone in the room digs into their bags and pulls out their calculators! *What? What is everyone doing? I don't understand the problem he just assigned!* The joke is on me. More than a few students shout out the answer, others confirming that they had figured it out as well.

Thankfully, the professor goes over the problem, outlines the formula, and writes the solution on the board. *Oh, boy, is this how it is going to go?* I am in over my head, and it is not even nine o'clock in the morning!

The rest of the class is a blur. I feverishly write everything down, resulting in pages of notes that I hope I can make sense of after class. There is no time to edit or think. Just write and worry about it later. Finally, to my relief, the professor announces the end of the class along with the assignments due before next week. My second wave of panic begins to set in. I'm overwhelmed by the amount of work needed to complete these assignments by next week. *How will I ever get this done? What was I thinking?*

As the room begins to clear, I sit for a minute to catch my breath before getting out of my seat. Slowly, I head back to the parking lot. Sitting in the safety of my car, I give myself a motivational talk. *"You can do this! You've overcome many obstacles before, and you'll do it again. Just keep moving forward."*

It's time to switch gears, and this is a workday. As I drive away from campus and head toward my first business appointment, I take a moment to remember the road I traveled to get here today. The long and winding road it took to get here.

SQUARE PEG IN A ROUND WORLD

As a child, my dream was to become a doctor. To my mind, a doctor was a healer, someone who genuinely cared about taking care of people. I still remember my second-grade book report on Elizabeth Blackwell, the first female physician in the United States. I enjoyed reading about her life and was intrigued to learn that she cared for sick patients dating back to the 1850s. She was a trailblazer and a doctor. That is what I was going to be! My hard work paid off. This book report earned me an "A."

One year, I received a toy doctor's bag for Christmas. I loved it and used the tools it held – a stethoscope, thermometer, and reflex hammer – to take care of my stuffed animals. I knew then that I would go to college and become the first woman doctor in my family. I did not realize at the time what a lofty dream it was. A dream that would not receive any nurturing at all.

In my home, higher education was never a priority – never valued. Neither of my parents graduated high school. My mother said she dropped out because her family moved so much, and she hated having to 'always be the new kid in class.' Her dream was to marry young, have children and be a homemaker. My dad left high school to help support his family by becoming an electrician. He and my mom met at a very young age, married, and quickly started their family.

I'm the oldest of three girls, three very well-behaved girls. We followed all the rules, were respectful, achieved good grades, and did our assigned chores. And there were always lots of assigned chores. My father believed that 'chores created the character.' In his view, it was essential to get them done quickly and correctly. Safe to say, Ann, Louise, and I were well on our way to having lots of character!

We each had a list of assigned jobs. The list was long, and yes, there were inspections. And yes, the lists were written out and posted on our bedroom walls. Saturday mornings were known as the dreaded Inspection Day. These inspections ensured we weren't slacking off (my father's phrase) and being sloppy. Dusting, as benign a chore as can be, would be followed by a white glove-style inspection, including the top of door jams, top of the refrigerator, and beneath the bed...we got the idea, the lesson to be absolutely thorough. Quite a lot to remember when you're ten years old!

Ann, Louise, and I quickly learned from our mistakes and made every effort not to make them twice. My dad had a wicked temper with a short fuse. None of us wanted to be the object of his fury. Best to do what you were told, stay quiet, and pray you didn't trigger his displeasure. Sadly, trying to anticipate from day to day what his displeasures and causes for irritation would be was always a crap-shoot. Again, quite a bit of stress to put on children's shoulders, but we did the best we could. If we failed to follow the rules, punishments were swift, severe, and all too frequent.

I usually passed my father's inspection. Even a drill sergeant would have been impressed by my military precision. My bed was always impeccably made. My room was spotless. And I always washed my breakfast dishes before I made my way to the bus stop.

My dad left for work before sunrise, so, at least before school, there was no immediate worry if my sisters and I unintentionally committed an infraction of the house rules. It was rare for us to see our mother before we left the house for school. Mom typically stayed in bed, too tired to get up that early – certainly too tired to make breakfast and send us to school. Let's say that she wasn't overly 'maternal.' Sleep was her priority, always the most important thing for her.

Although stressful, life was predictable for most of my early childhood. Things changed, however, when I turned twelve. My dad decided to start his own business, and the endeavor quickly became his focus. Money was tight, so hiring help was out of the question. He and my mother decided that she would work in the office every day, answer the phone, follow up with messages, and take care of the financial records.

My parents were opposites when it came to their drive to succeed, work, and achieve goals.

With a fantastic work ethic, my dad labored as an electrician during the day and built his own business by independently finding projects that he completed after hours. Sadly, my mother's work ethic was non-existent. She wasn't concerned about deadlines or returning phone messages. In her mind, there was always 'tomorrow.' It was apparent to me that she was not excited about this new business.

During this time, we rarely saw my dad. Before dawn, he left the house, to his "day job," then went straight to his evening jobs. He did not come home until after we were all in bed, getting only a few hours of sleep before starting it all over the next day. Sadly, I remember this as a calm, quiet, and enjoyable time in my life. Because Dad was not around, there were no 'infractions on the rules,' no way to trigger his temper. He no longer had the time or the energy for morning inspections. As for my mother, as long as she didn't have to do them, she never cared about chores.

Dad's hard work began to pay off, and after a while, his business grew. He had established himself as an excellent contractor, with a reputation for completing projects on time and within budget, with quality work resulting from his efforts. More projects meant more administrative support, which meant he needed more help in the office. So, he looked to me for help.

Along with making his life easier, my father felt that this was an excellent opportunity for me to learn organizational skills. He thought it was vital that I know how to draft and type letters, handle phone calls, prepare budgets, and order supplies for upcoming projects. In his mind, these were all essential skills that I needed to master to ensure the growth of his business.

Dad showed me how to type business letters, instructing me on attaching carbon paper so that when I removed a letter from the typewriter, it was pristine. No typing mistakes or sloppiness were ever acceptable. He coached me on returning phone messages professionally and promptly. We role-played phone calls, ensuring that I learned how to answer the phone with a friendly greeting and respond appropriately to callers. I needed to sound knowledgeable and professional, with authority but also respect. We practiced how to ask for bid packages and make notes for instructions on follow-up.

Over time, I began to assist with putting formal bid packages together. Attention to detail was essential; the numbers needed to be accurate. I began to take on more and more responsibility: working for an hour before going to school and returning to the home office after school, working until dinner time. Saturday was my full day in the office. An obvious bonus was that most of my chores were reassigned to my sisters so I could focus on office work – something they were not happy about.

At first, I was pleased to have so much responsibility and felt proud that my dad trusted me with such important work. After all, I had just turned thirteen. Over time, it became apparent that my mother was not putting in much effort during the day. She was often sick, always in a health crisis, or suffering from an ailment requiring many medications. Very little office work was done while I was at school. I understood that my mother was simply sleeping most of the day, arriving in the office just before I got home.

My solution was to work as quickly as I could, to take up Mom's slack. If my dad asked for something and it wasn't done when or how he expected, he would get angry – never a pleasant experience. When my dad came home, Mom and I were both at our desks, the two of us working diligently together in the office. This experience taught me how to be incredibly organized and incredible at multitasking!

As the years went on, my skills improved. I learned many lessons about building a business, becoming adept at meeting deadlines, creating business correspondence, balancing the checkbook, and coordinating project deadlines. What I was missing and yearning for was being a high school student. I wanted to participate in activities, wanted to try out for cheerleading, volleyball, or softball. Plus, in order to achieve my life-long goal of becoming a doctor, I would need to take some advanced math and science classes. My guidance counselor suggested that I get my parents' permission to sign up for these classes and then join a study group. The problem? The study groups met for an hour or so at the end of the school day, which would mean that I would not be available to work in my father's office in the afternoon.

Along with wanting to prepare for college, I wanted to be with my friends. I wanted to spend time with them after school, but I couldn't tell them why that was not possible. My dad was a very private and often very paranoid person. He thought that if I talked about his plans, he might lose his day job or opportunities to bid on other projects. None of my friends knew that I worked for him before school or spent long hours working after getting home. I couldn't tell my friends the truth about why I could not join them in attending any after-school events. Instead, I lied. I said I had to take care of my little sisters. I became practiced at keeping secrets, making excuses, and making them believable. After a while, most of my friends stopped asking. I did have a best friend, Maria, who lived down the street. She was the one person allowed to visit me at home because my father liked her. I treasured our friendship. Maria was kind and funny. And, although she did not ask many questions about my home life, I knew she knew it was a bit crazy.

I vividly remember getting up enough courage in my junior year of high school to ask if I could take some "time off from the office work." I wanted to try out for volleyball at school. My idea was to introduce the idea of my staying at school for a few hours in the afternoon. Once I did that, it might allow me time to attend a study group before having to report for practice. I spent a great deal of time strategizing my plan, writing out the details, and deciding to make my pitch at the dinner table. On the appointed evening, I could barely eat. My stomach was in knots, and I was praying that both of my parents would agree with my brilliant plan, the plan that I spent so much time on.

"Mom...Dad... I want to sign up for the volleyball team at school. Maria is trying out for the same team, and we can both attend the study group for advanced math and science classes on the same day as volleyball practice. We can walk home together, so you won't need to pick me up from school. I came up with a plan to work longer hours on Saturday and Sunday so that I can get all my work done. Being on the team will help me to be a better teammate. All of these things will help me to be more productive in the office."

I made my case, and I sat back in my seat. In my mind, this was brilliant! I could still accomplish my office duties AND have time for a study group and sports. How could my parents possibly disagree with such a masterful plan? Surely, this wasn't too much to ask!

Well... it was!

My father's response was immediate: How dare I assume that I could take "time off" and be so selfish. Bills needed to be paid, food needed to be put on the table, and spending time "goofing off with sports" was selfish and disrespectful to my family.

The tirade was loud and lasted for hours. Listening to it was exhausting. I was no stranger to being lectured. Lectures were my father's specialty. But this one was particularly harsh. I kept waiting for my mother to step in...take up my cause, plead my case. I waited in vain. After cleaning up, she left the kitchen: just me and him, and hours of angry words being hurled in my direction.

Later that evening, after the lecture finally ended, my mother came into my bedroom to make sure I was getting ready for bed. She also wanted to make sure I knew her opinion about my plan. She agreed with my father: I was selfish because my help was needed in the office. Sadly, I never asked for time off again.

Even more sadly, I began to see my mother in a different light. She was not going to advocate for me or support me in my dreams. The experience reinforced my feelings of isolation, of being different, of being an outsider. It cemented the thought that I didn't fit in. At school, I watched as my friends had fun, participating in sports and after-school gatherings; making plans and enjoying time together; even getting into some trouble; in other words, being teenagers. I realized that my life was not like my friends or any other teen I knew.

At the tender age of sixteen, my life centered on being successful at "work" – meeting business deadlines, creating accurate correspondence, and being responsible for earning an income to help our family. Instead of looking forward to high school sports, dances, activities, and dating, I was in training to be an office administrator. I felt utterly alone, unable to share my thoughts and disappointments with anyone – not even Maria. I knew it was best not to let her know. Not to let anyone know. In my mind and my heart, I knew I was a square peg in a round world.

COLLEGE DREAMS ON HOLD

I rarely remember my parents getting along, much less having fun. As a family, our outings were rare. Work was always the priority, and our home was a functional office for all intents and purposes. When work was going smoothly, it was peaceful at home. For me, I felt ready to take some risks and push a few boundaries.

Life is more exciting now. I have a boyfriend. Mr. Creativity is shy, handsome, and kind – and finishing up his senior year. Like most everything else in my life, the experience of having a boyfriend works differently for me than for my girlfriends. I'm not allowed to see anyone or to date. It is forbidden because it would interfere with my work in the family business.

But for the first time in my life, I decide to directly disobey orders. Mr. Creativity and I secretly make plans to meet. My best friend, Maria, is excited and helps cover for me. Mr. Creativity and I sneak away for a Sunday picnic lunch and hike. I love our time together, especially our walks. Mr. Creativity brings his camera, taking amazing photos of the trail scenery. His photographs are gorgeous, and I enjoy watching and learning from him. I love our time spent outdoors, appreciating the beauty of nature and the hours we spend talking.

Mr. Creativity is a sensitive soul, soft-spoken and exciting. He is often curious about my strict family rules, but he respects my hesitation in answering questions. I am aware of his growing protectiveness, and I have concerns that he may decide to get actively involved. He has openly said that "everyone knows your dad is a lunatic. If I find out he is hurting you, I will hurt him. Anything happens, and you give me a call."

I can see that he means it. I can see it in his eyes. It feels good to know that someone has my back. Finally, someone is in MY corner. But this? This is crazy talk. And Mr. Creativity has no idea just how crazy.

Like everything else in my life, I tell myself that I can manage Mr. Creativity. In a short time, I will graduate and head to college. Then Mr. Creativity and I plan to get an apartment. My life is starting to look up, and I let myself begin to feel happy!

It did not take long for my newfound happiness to crumble. During Sunday dinner, my parents announce their plans to separate and divorce. It is not a complete surprise to my sisters and me, but we quietly wonder what will happen next. We get our answer quickly: the turmoil, anger, and chaos are elevated and amplified.

It is also no surprise that my mother needs my help in making plans and finding an apartment. I know that time is of the essence, as the tension between my parents is volatile. My father has a girlfriend, and things will go nuclear if my mother finds out. I know that we need to get out now. So, I step up, do some research and schedule an appointment to visit an apartment located nearby, so my sisters and I won't have to change schools.

During the meeting with the rental manager, my mother signs the lease agreement, saying she will have to drop off the security deposit the next day. But, as we are driving home, Mom tells me that she does not have the money for the security deposit, asking if she can borrow it from me. How can she need my money? She is asking me for the money that I had painstakingly saved—my money for college. But in my family, my needs never mattered in the past. Why should they matter now? I give her all the money I have in the world, the money we need to secure the apartment.

Later that afternoon, my mother and I are in the kitchen. She is clear that she wants to move out, and thinks it is the best thing. The problem, she says, is that she wants to make sure that my father continues to support us financially. Mom does not feel it is her responsibility to get a job and take care of my sisters and me.

I'm livid. This move is the most important thing for all of us right now, a way to finally live in peace. My sisters and I certainly deserve it! I finally get up the nerve to ask, "Why are you deliberately making this difficult? You said that this is what you want, right? Why are you not happy about us moving out?"

"I don't answer to you," she growls, "you are the daughter. I am the mother." As she turns to leave the room, I yell back, "Then act like one!" I'm on a roll. "We have an apartment, and we are leaving, with or without you!" This new voice surprises me. Mom just turns and walks out of the room.

Here we are, finally in our new place. Ann, Louise, and I are so excited! My sisters and I quickly unpack our boxes and begin to set up our rooms. It is very cool to see them so happy! All three of us are sharing a small bedroom, but we do not care. We no longer have to endure long nights of endless arguing between my parents. Feeling a bit cramped pales in comparison to living happily, living in peace.

My father is busy creating a new life for himself. He rarely calls my sisters and me. He only phones my mother to argue about money. They still fight bitterly, but it is not as intrusive and easier to ignore because we only have to hear one side.

The tension between my mother and me has dissipated, and we discuss dividing up the finances. She thanks me for my help in getting us into the apartment and shares that she has found a job and will pay the rent. Whew… I am relieved. Finally, our lives will begin to calm down. Maybe I will even be able to enjoy the last few months left in my senior year. Plus, I am thrilled that I can finally spend time with Mr. Creativity without hiding; I can begin to live my life out loud! Just like my friends.

Mr. Creativity and I celebrate by going to dinner, where we optimistically make plans together. We have a terrific time, relaxing and laughing – neither of us looking over our shoulder in fear of getting caught on a date.

Our future feels secure. I will soon graduate high school and get a part-time job while I go to community college. Because I gave my mother all my money for the apartment deposit, I will need to save up before going to university. Mr. Creativity can support both of us, now that he has a full-time job. He has no interest in college and is happy to help me. I am so thankful to have him, someone who listens to me, who wants to take care of me. I have never felt this way before, and I love every minute of it!

The mood quickly shifts on Saturday morning when my mother comes into the kitchen. "I need you to sit down," she begins. "We have something that we need to talk about. I did get a job, but it is only part-time and does not pay enough to cover the rent. You will need to get a full-time job to help out."

I stop breathing. "Full-time job? You mean, quit high school and get a job?" I am sure that I misunderstand; this can't be what I am hearing. But my mother confirms my worst fear.

"Well…yeah. We need more income, and this is not a time for you to be selfish."

My ears burn, and my mouth is dry. I feel a volcano in my gut, ready to erupt. My heart is beating so fast that I think my chest will explode. "Are you crazy?" I shout. "Are you insane? I finally have a life … and you want me to quit school! In my senior year? I already gave up all my money to get us here. You need to get another job, get two jobs! That is what parents do … whatever they have to do to take care of their children."

Ann and Louise quickly come into the kitchen after hearing the commotion. They are both crying, their faces filled with fear, and they both offer to get part-time jobs to help out.

Mom continues, "Your grandmother will be moving in with us, and her pension will bring in extra income. I am telling you that in order to live in this house, you will live by my rules. YOU do not tell ME that I need to get another job. I tell YOU what to do!"

This argument is getting ugly, getting out of hand. I am so angry that my head hurts. I can't think, and I am blinded by rage and disbelief. What now? How can I make this work? How much more can I take? And when will this craziness stop?

I rush out of the room, my hands shaking as I dial the phone. After calmly listening to my rambling story, Mr. Creativity tells me to go outside and wait for him at the corner. I pour myself into his car, and we drive away. I realize that I can not speak in complete sentences. I am only able to get out a few nouns and verbs. The fact that he pieces together the story is a testament to his care and patience. We drive to his parent's house, where I am finally able to calm down. Sitting at their dining room table, we decide that we will get a place of our own. It is sooner than we planned, but I melt as he gives me a big hug and tells me that everything will be alright. We sit for a while, in silence. I begin to believe him.

TENACIOUS PURSUIT OF A FAMILY

"A re you ready? It's time for us to go, or we will be late."

Mr. Creativity is getting impatient. It is taking me some time to get dressed and moving this morning. I drag myself from the bathroom, slowly making my way to the living room. It is pouring rain outside – that February-cold rain that chills me right to my bones. The gray morning matches my mood. I am sick and tired of feeling sick and tired.

Finally, heeding everyone's advice, I am going to the doctor. *What's going on? Is this something serious? Do I have the flu? Is it cancer? Or am I just lazy?*

My mind continues to race on the drive to my doctor's office. I am sure he will tell me that I only have the flu. My physician since childhood, Dr. Frey, is a gentle soul and would never scold me for wasting his time. I hope so.

He walks into the exam room, asking me to come into his office. "Bring your boyfriend in. We can all talk together."

Now I panic! *I'm right; it is horrible news!* In Dr. Frey's small windowless office, I focus on his walls lined with diplomas. I read and study them like I am preparing for an exam—anything to remain calm.

"My dear," Dr. Frey begins, "the tests reveal that you are going to have a baby."

The world stops. I look over to Mr. Creativity and see the color drain from his face. My mouth is dry as I ask my doctor, "Are you sure?" I want to be sure I heard correctly. Yes, the test was positive. "Congratulations, you are going to be a mother!"

Congratulations? I am nineteen, living with my boyfriend in an apartment no bigger than a bread box. Neither of us has any money. And now we are going to be parents? I want to be happy. But fear, panic, angst, and worry crash over me like ocean waves. And with my nausea, I do not need any more waves. Dr. Frey gives us a referral to an obstetrician and asks that we make an appointment for prenatal care as soon as possible. Somehow, I find the strength to thank him as Mr. Creativity and I head toward the door. I walked into this office fearing I had a terrible disease, and I am leaving with a baby. What a day this has turned out to be!

As we walk to the parking lot, I see that Mr. Creativity is smiling. I can't help but ask, "Aren't you at all nervous?"

"No! I am going to be a dad!" He unlocks my side of the car and helps me into my seat. Chivalry is not dead.

Driving home, Mr. Creativity expands on his optimistic view. "Who cares about the money? We will make it work! We both have jobs, and we will save our money. The baby is due in November, so we have plenty of time."

By my calculation, that is only seven months away – not my idea of plenty of time. My mind is racing again. Until today, the money we budgeted for savings was supposed to help me reach my goal of going to community college. I begin imagining the comments from family and friends: "She moves in with her boyfriend, has a little freedom, and look what happens ... she ends up pregnant, the poor thing." My life is now a cliché.

Mr. Creativity reaches over and touches my hand, telling me that he is both nervous and excited, telling me that we will face this together. This is oddly comforting. *Face it together*. That sounds great to me. Not having to do this on my own is a new experience.

At home, sitting at the table in our tiny kitchen, we make plans to share the big news with our families. The smile on his face disappears as he says, "I think it is better for me to meet with my parents by myself. They may not see this as good news, and I am not sure how they will react." We both grew up in the Catholic faith. But his mother and father are very devout, while my family only attends church on important religious holidays. "I do not want to worry that they say something to upset you. It may take a while for them to accept this."

We agree that we will meet with our families separately, hoping that makes it easier for everyone to process this news. Tomorrow, our parents will learn that they will soon be grandparents. They will certainly be surprised!

⁂

Mr. Creativity gives me a big hug and kiss as we both head out the door. "Good luck, drive safe," he says as I unlock the car door. We both head off to deliver the news of our baby to our respective families. I am nervous and still sick to my stomach. My mother and I continue to have a strained relationship. I have never found her to be maternal or supportive of me, but I hope today will be different. I need this to go well. I have had enough angst and upset in my life.

I decide to stop and order food. *Bringing lunch for my mother and sisters is an excellent way to cushion the news.* Making my way into the parking lot, I begin to encourage myself. *Why would my mother be upset? I live on my own, not with her. I am bringing her news of her first grandchild, and she will be happy. She will be shocked at first, then delighted.*

Arriving at my mother's house, I gather up my courage along with the bags of take-away food and walk toward her front door. We chit-chat over lunch. I do my best to assess her mood, but my anxiety is building, and I can not wait any longer. My heart is pounding so hard I can barely breathe. My stomach is in knots, adding to my nausea. *Just get this over with, like ripping off a bandage. Just tell her your big news.* My voice cracks as I begin, "Mom, I have some news ... I went to the doctor yesterday, and he told me that I am pregnant."

My mother, as usual, does not move. She sits stoically in her seat. Then, "I hope you know that this is your responsibility. You need to know two things: first, I am not a babysitter. Second, you are not moving back into my house. You two need to figure this out." With that, she leaves the room.

Part of me expected her reaction. Part of me was hoping that she would wrap her arms around me and tell me that it will all be alright. I want her support, especially now. I am nervous, scared, and need my mother's comfort. I realize that I have a vision that my news will somehow bring us together in my mind's eye. After all, she was a young mother herself. But, as always, she thinks only of herself. Hearing my information, she immediately thinks only of how this may disrupt HER life; no surprises here. She is nothing but consistent, the epitome of self-centeredness and a shining example of what I do not want to become. I decide that I won't be like her. My child will always feel love, comfort, and support.

I run to my car and drive home in a daze. I close the door behind me, pour myself into bed, and close my eyes. I am exhausted. Mr. Creativity is not home yet, and I wonder how things are going for him. Letting out a deep breath, I go to the kitchen for some crackers to settle my stomach, ending up on our lumpy second-hand sofa in our compact living room. I can hear myself crying, unable to stop. The enormity of the past few days has taken its toll. How fitting that I am once again alone, figuring out how to move forward in the face of a huge challenge.

Finally, the father-to-be arrives home and shares how it went with his family. "They were surprised and asked if we were getting married." He tells me they all talked about our plans, his mother and father doing their best to be supportive. As he is talking, the phone rings. Saying, "It is for you," he hands me the phone. *Who would be calling me? My mother? Does she want to reach out and apologize? Say that we will figure this out together?*

"We heard the news," his mother begins, "and want you to know that we are here for you both. Come to dinner on Sunday, and we can talk about your plans." I thank her for her kindness and understanding and assure her that we will be there on Sunday.

I need to process this. His mother calls me to tell me that she supports us, while my mother tells me we are on our own. Mr. Creativity and I make our way to the sofa, and he hugs me tightly. "This is going to work out, you will see."

We decide to marry. It is essential for his parents that we have a church wedding. Though initially disappointed with our news, they have given both of us fantastic support and understanding, making every effort to welcome me into their family. His parents decide to pay for our June wedding, followed by a small reception. While happy that we are getting married, my mother makes it very clear that she has no plans – or ability – to contribute financially to the celebration.

I enjoy spending time with my new family. My mother-in-law-to-be is kind and caring. For the first time, a positive mother influences my life, and I realize that I have always wanted to be part of a loving family. And now I am.

While there was no formal discussion, my mother and I somehow find ourselves in 'truce mode.' I make an effort to include her, with no expectations at all. Part of me wants to exclude her. But that would result in the exclusion of my sisters, and I wanted to have some of my family at my wedding!

My mother announces that she wants to be the one to purchase my wedding dress. I smile and thank her – as she shares that she found a wedding dress in the newspaper. *Newspaper? Aren't we going to share the experience of a trip to the bridal salon and trying on all of the gorgeous wedding dresses?* I am sad and disappointed – hoping I misunderstood.

Nope. We drive to the address in the newspaper and arrive home with the dress I will wear. Interestingly, my mother buys a new outfit for herself – including new shoes. I am not sure where she finds the money for all of this, but it represents my mother's total contribution to my wedding. I remind myself that I have no expectations, telling myself she is simply incapable of changing her behavior. I just want to be at peace, to enjoy this time in my life. And it works for now.

The sun shining into our bedroom wakes me on this beautiful June morning– my wedding day. I decide to concentrate on being happy and grateful today. I will enjoy all the festivities his parents have arranged for us. We will all have such fun, with lots of laughter and dancing. Today, I have no worries. By this afternoon, I'll be a wife and mother-to-be. Luckily, my dress hides any evidence of our bundle of joy.

It turns out to be a festive day, with plenty of laughter and joy. My mother and sisters enjoy themselves. Mr. Creativity's family made it possible for all of us to feel like an extended family. I will always be very grateful to them for that.

It is Halloween. We are heading to my scheduled doctor's visit, now part of our weekly routine. My due date is fast approaching, and we are both so excited. We have been busy with preparations for the baby's arrival. My sister-in-law hosted the most beautiful baby shower, and we received many unique gifts. In addition to throwing the shower, she bought us an elegant wooden baby crib, its canopy laced with gauzy white fabric. Although it takes up most of the space in our bedroom, we don't care. It is the most beautiful piece of furniture we own. My mother and sisters gave us cute clothes, and my mother crocheted a stunning baby blanket made of the softest white yarn I had ever touched. Everything was coming together for all of us. Mr. Creativity and I wake up each morning and instinctively look into the empty crib. Almost time for our little one to arrive. Almost time.

꙳

Dr. Cimina says my blood pressure has risen to the point of concern. "We feel the best plan is to admit you and begin to induce labor this evening." *Today? I am not ready today. It is Halloween, and we have to be home to give out candy to all of the trick-or-treaters.* Our obstetrician goes on to tell us, "While we have some concerns, I expect everything to go well. It looks like you will be a mommy by tomorrow." *Okay. I take a deep breath. Tomorrow, Tuesday, November 1st, I will be a mommy.*

That was our doctor's plan. My baby, it seems, has other ideas. My little one is not ready, not ready at all. Four days of labor, four days without my baby. Finally, our son decides to arrive on Thursday evening, November 5th. Finally, we get to meet James, our beautiful little boy! We looked at him and decide we will call him Jim. Welcome to our family, Jim.

I want this moment to be like what I used to see in the movies. I wanted this joyful moment to lead to my 'happily ever after.' Sadly, it would not be.

❧

The pressure of becoming parents, of supporting ourselves and a baby on minimal wages results in overwhelming stress and failure. We do our best to make things work. But we are two completely different people. Mr. Creativity is a great dad but not a great provider. In any sense of the word. He does not like to work, finds the concept of money 'boring.' My tenacious pursuit of a family is fading away. And ultimately, we decide to divorce.

We agree that I will have primary custody of our son. As it is 'blood is thicker than water,' he gets custody of his mother. She is not at all pleased with our decision. She completely supports her son and places blame directly on me. Our relationship permanently fractures. Sadly, I am losing my husband and my mother-in-law.

And so, here I go again – making plans to create a new life at age twenty. This time as a single mom. I now need to focus on finding a job that will support us both. Jim depends on me, and I am determined to figure this out, just like I always do. I do not have a choice. A crash course in life, coming up. Oddly, this is familiar territory for me. *Onward I go!*

COLLEGE GOALS REVISITED

I have been managing pretty well over the past couple of years, and I have been able to secure a full-time job. Thankfully, I have plenty of opportunities to work extra hours, which is often necessary to help with my rent. Mr. Creativity helps with child support when he can, but that is not too often as he has a spotty work history. His on-again, off-again employment gives him plenty of time to spend with our son, and he does, thankfully, take care of him while I work. Sharing custody allows me to work overtime without paying a babysitter. Mr. Creativity promised me that we would 'be in this together.' Little did I know at the time that he did not mean financially.

His family, as always, pitches in to help take care of Jim. They support their son and are totally in love with their grandson. Jim is a curious child, an absolute delight. He is happy and enjoys spending the day having fun with his dad. They are always busy, taking trips to the park or zoo. At times I feel a bit sad, wishing I could spend the same time with Jim. But one of his parents has to be financially responsible. I must take care of this beautiful little boy. I do not have the luxury of finding money "boring."

Despite all of this, things shift into a rhythm. I am managing motherhood, my finances, my tiny apartment, and my job. While there isn't much time for a social life, I am still pleased with my success. A small promotion at work means I won't have to depend on overtime, affording me some much-needed free time.

What another fun night! It feels so nice to have someone take me to dinner and show interest in me! Being a single mom has not been easy. My new beau, Mr. Personality, and I have known each other for many years – exchanging pleasantries when we crossed paths at work. He went through his divorce years before me and has children of his own. Although he is older than me, we joke that I am 'mature beyond my years' and he is 'immature for his.' We enjoy each other's company, and he tells me he appreciates my 'moxie.'

In no time at all, Mr. Personality introduces me to his mother and father. They are lovely people, and they appreciate the fact that I financially support my son by myself at such a young age. After meeting me, his parents give their approval – an essential milestone in our relationship. They were not pleased to hear their thirty-eight-year-old son is dating a twenty-two-year-old divorcee – with a two-year-old child, no less. But Mr. Personality and Jim get along famously and have fun when they are together. Next on the agenda: have our children meet each other. No hurdles, just smooth sailing. It is easy to visualize the makings of my new family.

After failed marriages for both of us, we decide to move in together and create a home for our newly blended family. The structure of our relationship begins to take shape, with Mr. Personality taking the lead. Perhaps because he is older, I look to him as the 'wiser one.'

At his insistence, we keep our accounts separate. As I am solely responsible for my son, Mr. Personality does not want my ex-husband to think that he will financially take care of my Jim. I will contribute to our monthly household expenses, and we will each take care of our respective children. *A red flag?* I ignore it, convincing myself that this is what it takes to be part of this new family. I want us – my son and me – to experience being part of a family. No longer an only child, he now has siblings. Everyone gets along and loves one another. I feel like I just hit the jackpot.

☙

Our lives are busy. We make time for each other and time with our children, taking them on family vacations, cruises, and to the Caribbean. While I am happy with my blended family, I am yearning for a commitment. After seven years, I want to be married. I am finding my voice as I get older, and I begin to make demands, pushing for my vision of what I want in this family.

Luckily, Mr. Personality's parents and our respective children feel the same way. After much discussion – and stalling on his part – I put my foot down and set a wedding date. If he does not want to commit and get onboard, I am moving out. It is time. I want to set an example for our children. He finally agrees, and we move forward, full steam ahead.

The children have fun with the wedding planning. Jim, now nine years old, is beyond excited about his new tuxedo. All of our children will be part of the ceremony. Mr. Personality's parents are pleased. Thanks to our improved relationship and enduring truce over the last few years, I am at peace with my mother and looking forward to spending time with my sisters and their families at the wedding. I have lost touch with my father and have no plans to get back in touch, ever.

Even as we prepare for marriage, Mr. Personality remains adamant about keeping our finances separate. To protect his children, he also insists on a prenuptial agreement, telling me that I should understand his reasoning as he has more financial assets than me. *Another red flag?* I ignore this one, too, and convince myself that I do not want to appear to be a gold digger. I am contributing a significant portion of my finances to this new family and, although I have some doubts, I decide that this marriage will be for the rest of our lives, making this prenup a non-issue. So, sign it, I do.

A couple of years pass as I continue to successfully build my career. Being in sales gives me the ability to increase my income and earn decent bonuses. I am doing well selling office equipment and preparing for a position with higher income potential. In reality, I am bored selling office equipment alongside immature 'just out of college' young men. Their stories of bar nights, late dates, and childish pranks are getting old. I am the only woman in my office, working alongside twenty-five frat boys. I do not fit in with this group. But, other sales positions are challenging without a college degree – if not impossible – to attain.

My new goal? Medical sales. My dream of becoming a physician may now be out of reach, but it would be rewarding to work with medical practitioners, providing products that support patient care. I am focused on this goal; calling on hospitals is my new dream. I am working with several sales recruiters, but they are less than optimistic about my ability to secure a medical sales position with my background: specifically, my lack of a formal education.

Thankfully, a dear friend of mine, Sheila, tells me of a position in a new start-up company. She just signed on with the company, which needs another representative to cover the geography where I live.

Sheila provides an excellent reference, enough to get me the interview.

I meet the owner and chief financial officer sitting in a conference room, who ask about my background. "We know that you came highly recommended," the owner says. "However, we are concerned about your lack of formal education. We sell to and educate clinicians, and we must ensure that you are up to the task. We are sorry to say that we do not see this job as a good fit for you. We believe that a college education is a minimal requirement for this position."

Are you kidding me? Not sure I am up to the task? I tell myself that now is the time to be bold, to outline my plan, the plan that I have spent so much time working out. I need to show them that I deserve this job! I take a deep breath, look them both directly in the eye, and begin to speak (praying that my voice doesn't quiver).

"I understand your trepidation. Let me assure you that I have given this a great deal of thought, and I would like to share my plan to succeed. First, we can agree to a ninety-day trial period. Within that ninety days, I will enroll in community college and take anatomy and physiology courses, enabling me to acquire the knowledge I need to sell your medical products. Additionally, before my first day, I will accompany Sheila on her sales calls and learn how to set up a territory. This ensures that my training takes place on my own time, with my own money. If I do not meet your goals and objectives after the trial period, you can let me go. I know I can quickly learn product features and benefits and be successful in selling your medical products. What can't be taught – in my view – are motivation, tenacity, and passion. You either have them, or you don't. As it so happens, I have them. I am self-motivated, a quick learner, and committed to achieving success."

I wait for a moment, take another breath, and decide to just 'go for it.' In a voice I do not recognize, I ask, "What do you have to lose?" And my big finish, "Plus, look at what you have to gain. I am the right person for this job, and I am asking for the chance to prove it."

The room is silent. I sit nervously in my chair, hoping they won't see my knees shaking under the table. I want to appear calm, cool, and in charge. They do not speak, and just glance at each other. The owner jots notes on the pad in front of him and gets up from his chair. He shakes my hand, walks me to the door, and tells me they will be in touch. I thank them for their time and say that I look forward to hearing from them; I appreciate being considered for the position, and I would love to join their team. As I slowly walk to the elevator and press the button, I think, *Did I blow it? Are they pleased, impressed?* I have no idea. The interview begins to play over and over in my head as the elevator doors slowly close.

What an excellent phone call! Just one week after my interview, I learn I have the job, and my start date is two weeks away! Finally, my life is turning around! I am excited to move forward and work with medical professionals! Frankly, I am not sure what is more exciting – hearing that I have a new medical sales position or realizing I get to enroll in school!

Keeping to my plan, I drive to the community college accompanied by my course catalog, with the anatomy and physiology classes I need to take highlighted in neon yellow. Nervously, I make my way to the admissions office. I love walking into the building, knowing that I will soon be a student – that I will soon belong here! I enroll, barely containing my excitement! l. I feel like I am walking on air. I just registered for college!

At dinner, I share my great news with Mr. Personality and my son. Jim begins to question my decision, "You *want* to go to school, Mommy? You know they give you lots of homework, right?"

I can't stop smiling, oozing enthusiasm, "I know, and I can not wait!"

Jim continues to look puzzled and shakes his head. Mr. Personality echoes my son's statement, albeit for a different reason. He chimes in, "Yes, you will have a lot of homework. How will you manage all of your schoolwork and a demanding job *and* take care of this family?"

My excitement begins to wane. I assure them both that I can do it all and change the subject. No one is going to dampen my mood today.

I love being in the classroom setting, learning about the human body. Looking around, I notice that most of the students are obviously just out of high school and appear to be heading to nursing and medical school. I silently reassure myself that it does not matter; I am here!

The classes are challenging, as are the assignments. I create flashcards that I can review in between sales calls and after dinner. Mr. Personality continues to make his feelings clear: he is unhappy with my new academic endeavor. As it becomes apparent that the only way to continue at school is to get everything done at home, I fall back on my multi-tasking abilities.

After I start dinner, I put in a load of laundry and finish cleaning the house, quickly running from job to job, quieting all the buzzers and timers. I feel as if I need roller skates to keep up. But if I need to run through my house like a crazy person to satisfy Mr. Personality, that's what I will do. It is all worth it. I keep picturing graduation day – the pride, the joy, the sense of accomplishment. That is what I choose to focus on. Jim and my husband will be proud of me then. *Just keep going, Carla. Just keep going.*

Having had a successful first semester, I decide to continue going to school. I can't wait to enroll again; microbiology is the next class on my schedule. However, juggling school, work, and motherhood on top of being a wife is a tall order. Mr. Personality seems to go out of his way to point out that I am not attentive to him or Jim. Snide comments and eye rolls that follow every mention of school, along with constant household disruption, are now part of our daily routine. Disagreements and arguments are more frequent and tiresome. *It is just school, what is the big deal? If going to school brings me so much joy, why is it such a problem? It is college; I am not gambling or staying out all night drinking, for goodness' sake!*

My job becomes more demanding, requiring mandatory out-of-town business meetings. I have an overnight trip coming up, so I make time to hit the grocery store on my way home. I prepare a couple of meals and put them in the refrigerator for the "boys" before departing. Exhausted, I head upstairs to pack. Mr. Personality walks in the room, annoyed. "School is interfering with family time; you never have time for us anymore. You are always exhausted, always busy." But his tirade isn't finished. "I am not sure why you need to finish these classes. You already have a great job, and you are making good money." And then, unbelievably, "Enough is enough. I think you should quit."

Quit? You think I should quit? I am furious.

"I am doing everything you ask me to do! I love going to school, I am paying for it myself, and I have not stopped taking care of my son or you, have I? Why can't you support me? What is your problem?" I realize that my voice is shrill. We are heading for an argument that I do not have the time or energy for right now. So, I finish packing my bag and head back downstairs, deciding that sleeping on the sofa will allow me some peace. At least for tonight.

The tension in the house is overwhelming. Making matters worse, my job requires more overnight trips, which impacts my ability to attend classes. Mandatory work meetings make it impossible for me to attend my weekly compulsory lecture and lab classes. It is becoming impossible to juggle both work and studies, and after a couple of semesters, I realize that I need to choose: quit my job or withdraw from school.

Mr. Personality makes it clear that he does not support my quitting my job. He feels it is unfair of me even to ask. I am heartbroken. I find being a student rewarding and exhilarating. It brings me so much joy. Why can't I make him see that this means so much to me? I even offer to 'borrow' the money from him to complete my program, telling him I will pay him back with interest. He won't hear of it. Realizing that my dream of graduating is quickly fading away and is no longer a possibility makes me sick. My sadness is overwhelming, and my disappointment is palpable.

I walk out of my advisor's office, my withdrawal paperwork in hand. I have to accept that my college dream is now gone. Mr. Personality, on the other hand, is smiling and happy. He can't tell me enough how this is "beneficial" for all of us.

Beneficial for all of us? It certainly does not benefit me. Why can't I get him to understand how important this is to me? Sitting quietly in my room, I ask the recurring question. *Now what, Carla? Now what?*

MY NEW BEST FRIEND

My decision to end my marriage to Mr. Personality was a difficult one. We'd invested close to sixteen years of our lives together, but we both wanted different things. Ultimately, I wanted to have a stronger voice in our relationship. We could not seem to make that shift. Early in our relationship, it did not seem to matter. But, as I moved out of my twenties and into my thirties, I wanted to stop putting everyone else first and explore my life goals and purpose. Sadly, Mr. Personality was unable and unwilling to make our marriage a true partnership. Our focus had always been on what he wanted and what he thought. It was time for my life to be the priority. On a quiet Friday morning, over coffee, we realized that separation was inevitable. I began looking for a new place that afternoon.

Jim and I are settling into our new home. He is starting his senior year of high school, and we are constantly arguing about everything. He is restless. He does not like school, and he is not sure if he wants to attend college. He is also not sure if he wants to work. Frankly, he is not sure about anything. The one thing he is absolutely clear about is that I always seem to say the wrong thing.

I insist that college is mandatory if he wants to continue living in my house. I stress the importance of setting an academic foundation, how that foundation leads to increased career choices. I speak from experience and, although he disagrees, Jim is at least exploring the possibility of attending community college for at least one semester. While I find exhilaration and happiness in the classroom, Jim finds school tedious and frustrating. He is out with his friends this evening, and I decide to do the same.

Doing my best to wait patiently at a red light, I see my best friend, Maria, turning into the restaurant's parking lot. I am looking forward to catching up with her. Maria has always been, and continues to be, a true bestie, supporting me throughout my life. We still laugh about how much our lives have changed since we met in first grade. We would often talk through the years about what our life plans were going to be "when we grow up." At the age of thirty-seven, she is working on her doctorate, with graduation not far away. And I am twice divorced. That wasn't part of my life's dream. And yet ... Here I am.

Just before the light turns green, out of the corner of my eye, I notice the person in the car next to me waving, trying to get my attention. I glance over and recognize an old childhood friend. As I roll down my window, he smiles and says, "I thought that was you, Carla! How are you? Where are you headed?"

It is good to see him; it has been a while. "Just over here at the restaurant, meeting Maria for dinner." The light changes, and he quickly shouts, "Great, I have an appointment nearby. If I finish up early, I will stop in and see you both."

I park the car and sit for a moment. Seeing Mr. Wonderful triggers childhood memories that come flooding back. He and I always had a close connection, growing up in the same neighborhood. We enjoyed spending time together in high school, and even I thought he would be my first serious boyfriend. I had not figured out how to maneuver the strict rules my father mandated, so we were never able to set up proper dates. He moved on and dated other girls. He is just as handsome as ever!

I begin to wonder what he has been doing these last years. The latest news I heard had him engaged, although that was a few years back. I hope he joins us; it would be great to see him again.

I tell Maria that I just ran into Mr. Wonderful at the traffic light. "Not literally," we both laugh, "but he may stop by if he can. I really hope he does."

Opening her menu, Maria agrees, "That would be great! I have not seen him in a while myself. Let's order some wine and appetizers to start." She read my mind. We want this to be a night to relax and catch up. The drinks arrive, and our spicy girl talk begins. I almost forgot how wonderful it is to laugh with your girlfriends.

In no time at all, appetizers arrive; so does Mr. Wonderful. "Ladies, did you order enough for me?" We laugh and place our food order. The three of us are having a great dinner – life-long friends sharing the details of our busy lives. I offer up news of my second, disastrous divorce, and he offers the story of his canceled engagement. After all the lousy news updates, we spend time reminiscing about the 'old days.' It is such fun, a welcome respite from these last months and years. Over coffee, we decide that we will do this again.

Before I get into my car, Mr. Wonderful asks me if I would like to have lunch with him next week. I smile and accept. On my way home, I can not contain my excitement, belting out songs on the radio like I am singing at Carnegie Hall. I am like a teenager again, feeling an incredible spark of attraction – and wondering if Mr. Wonderful feels the same way.

We are deep into our weekly lunch salads when we talk about our past relationships. We assure each other we will take things slow and not rush this relationship. Mr. Wonderful is busy with his career, never married, or had children. The conversation is easy and engaging. There is a comfort to this relationship. I enjoy his wicked sense of humor, and we laugh often.

My son knows Mr. Wonderful well, so there is no need for formal family introductions. Meals at his parent's home are fun and familiar, with shared stories about when we were 'kids.' I get along well with his mom and dad and find myself spending more time with them – especially enjoying the time I spend with his mom. She makes it clear. She is pleased with our budding romance.

Taking things slow was our plan. Instead, we quickly move along, each relishing the experience of a friendship turning into romance. Mr. Wonderful and I share a desire to be in a committed relationship. I share that my ex-husband never supported me or my dreams – specifically, my dream of going back to school. Mr. Wonderful finds that puzzling and agrees that partners should help one another. Music to my ears: he is aware of my past but doesn't fault me for my mistakes. Our life goals and plans are in sync.

Before long, we decide to share a home. Both my son and his family are supportive. Jim will live with us while he attends community college. It is a fantastic time. Mr. Wonderful purchases a house with a pool to become a home base for family and friends. Summers are full of fun, with numerous barbecues and parties. My son welcomes hearing another voice, a male voice, when discussing his plans. Lots of testosterone in this house!

Soon, though, Jim is packing, preparing to transfer to a four-year Southern university a couple of states away. I am very proud of him. It took a couple of semesters at the community college to find an area of study he finds interesting, and he is moving forward with a focus on business. He will be renting a room in an off-campus house and, even though he declined my offer of help, I can see that he is nervous. I pack a cooler for the long ride to his new place. There are so many things that I want to say, but every time I try to begin, he shuts me down.

"Let him figure this out on his own," Mr. Wonderful tells me. "He is trying to distance himself from being a child to becoming a man." Although Mr. Wonderful is trying to help me understand, Jim will always be my child. Maybe I am the nervous one. I have been looking forward to this day, the day my baby would leave the nest and make his way into the world. But I am quite sad and melancholy. Now that the day is here, I am not ready. I replay his childhood years in my mind. I wanted him to have a happy family, one that was loving and supportive. Guilt and embarrassment often creep in when I think about how my son had to endure two divorces, resulting in the elimination of growing up in a traditional nuclear family.

"I'm ready to go, Ma. The last thing to put in the car is the cooler." Jim gives me a big hug, and I begin to cry.

"Please drive carefully and take your time. Call me when you get there. I love you so much." He smiles, agreeing to call me. Frankly, I know that he will forget – he always does. Standing on the porch, I watch him drive away. My baby boy is gone.

Before the day gets away from me, I straighten up the house. Passing by his room, I notice a small envelope on his dresser, addressed to me. I sit down on his bed and begin to read the thoughts he chose to express in writing, beautifully, eloquently, and in his own words. This letter touches my heart. He is a gifted writer. As I work my way through an entire box of tissues, I can't feel any prouder. I already miss him terribly.

Sitting in his room, I let the emptiness and silence sink in. Now that he is on his own, I wonder if it is time to go after my dream; go back to college. Why not go back and finally get my four-year degree? Hmmm…

A DREAM REALIZED

Soon after Jim left for college, I decided to pursue my long-standing dream of higher education. It was my goal to attend college immediately after high school. A few decades later, I transferred my community college credits to the University of Maryland, Baltimore County, as a biology major. My dream university! I planned on graduating in two years.

I love spending time researching the process for applying and attending college. I am so excited that I share my plan with Mr. Wonderful over dinner, hoping he will be as enthusiastic as I am.

After a long silence, he says, "Well, money is a concern for me. I am worried that it will create a burden on our finances. We are finally at a place where we can enjoy life, and you want to saddle yourself with school."

Good grief, not again! What changed? Red flag? I ignore it; this is just too important to me. I want to scream and shake my finger in his face. *Keep your cool, stick to your plan.* "I know it will cost quite a bit of money, but my income from my medical sales job will pay for my son's college tuition *and* my tuition. My job is less demanding and requires less travel, so attending classes should not be a problem." I take a deep breath. "This is something I really want to do. I would like you to support me, as I always support you."

He reluctantly agrees and says that he needs to get back to work for an evening appointment. I am mildly disappointed and slightly irritated by Mr. Wonderful's lack of enthusiasm. But, as always, I move forward.

I stalk the mailbox daily, waiting for the envelope from the University. By the time I receive the letter confirming my status as a transfer student, I am already making plans for my first day!

I struggle to keep up with my classes. Chemistry and Biology are ridiculously challenging. Adding to my stress level is the announcement that we will be working with partners in our weekly chemistry labs. This is the dreaded morning, the day we select our lab partners. The professor begins to announce the partnerships. The room is silent, and the tension in the air is as thick as fog. No eye contact was made. Everyone is praying they are not the last student standing. After my team is announced, my partner walks over. I am grateful that she takes the initiative and introduces herself, telling me she graduated high school a year earlier than expected and planned to attend medical school. She is an academically gifted, mature, and lovely young woman.

"You are a very bright young lady, and I completely understand if you want to ask for another chemistry partner, someone sharing your academic skills. I do not want to hold you back," I tell her. "I will do my best to do my fair share and contribute to our team."

She smiles, "I don't think that is necessary. We will make this work. Everyone is learning; we can learn together." I am not entirely relieved, and I do my best to believe her.

Labs are torture. I feel awkward in this space, afraid that I will break a beaker or mix the wrong reagents, drawing attention to myself. I have nightmares that I will cause an unexpected explosion in the chemistry lab and make the evening news. My partner, on the other hand, is completely comfortable. Out of my element, I finish each week more depressed than the week before.

Before our first exam, my partner and I create flashcards to help us memorize all of the equations and formulas. As we are walking to the parking lot after packing up, she stops and says, "My mom and I were talking, and she said to tell you that she thinks what you are doing is great. She is impressed that you are taking this class." I thank her and ask her to pass my gratitude to her mother. Opening my car door, I turn around and look at the chemistry building. *How am I ever going to do this? Am I crazy?* For so long, I have wanted to be here, to be a student. But I am a fish out of water, way out of water. Sighing, I head to work, praying that I do well on my exam.

Time has not been my friend. Things have gone from bad to worse. The material is beyond challenging, and my grades are proof. I constantly berate myself that I am blowing my chance to finish school and decide to request a meeting with my academic advisor.

Mr. Sebastian and I have talked a few times already. He is a compassionate man and loves supporting students in their academic goals. During those previous conversations, Mr. Sebastian assured me that many students struggle in new classes. "Learning is a process, he said, and asked questions that helped me focus on my vision for my future and helped me identify courses that interested me. His sincerity and support are genuine, and he puts me at ease.

Today, walking through his door, I feel like a child going to see the principal. Mr. Sebastian is shuffling papers on his desk, pulling out my file so he can make some notes when I start the conversation.

"I have given this a lot of thought, and I think it is best that I withdraw from the University before I fail the program. The classes are challenging, and my grades are embarrassing. No matter how much time I devote to preparation, I am still failing." I do my best to hide the quiver in my voice, the tears suddenly welling up. *You are not a kid. You are a forty-something successful medical sales representative, getting ready to cry in your academic advisor's office.* To say that I feel embarrassed would be an understatement.

He listens to my story but does not immediately respond. *He agrees with me!* He begins moving paper on his desk. *He is getting ready to find the paperwork for me to sign.* Now I am mortified!

"Carla," he begins, "I believe you have a couple of choices. The classes *are* challenging, even for students fresh out of high school. Many of them have already taken advanced chemistry, biology, and math classes before attending their freshman year here. It has been a while since you attended school. You do not have a foundation for these advanced classes. It has nothing to do with your intelligence. It has to do with preparation. You can withdraw from these classes and take some foundational courses that could help you advance through the program. Or you can change your major to one that supports your goals and matches your interests and skills."

Wait! Is he saying there is another option? Is he giving me hope that I can successfully finish school? I move forward in my chair, focused on every word he is saying. We agree my goal of becoming a physician is not realistic. Not now. "What is it about being a doctor that speaks to you? What is it that you would do as a doctor?" he asks.

These are two excellent questions that I have not thought about before, and that intrigue me. "I love the idea of working with people on their health goals, partnering with them, and finding ways in which they can feel better. I want to be a resource, a voice, an advocate for people struggling with illness."

A brief moment of silence. Then, "I have suspected as much after our conversations. Passion, compassion, and empathy are all part of your skillset. So, let us find a program that allows you to build on those skills. We have a program focusing on health administration and policy that prepares students for administrative positions in hospitals, healthcare facilities, nonprofit organizations, and government organizations focused on health policy and healthcare delivery. Given your background, talent, ambition, and goals—I think it is a perfect fit." *How did I miss this? It is a perfect fit and tailor-made for me!*

We spend some time going over the study plan and make all of the arrangements to change my major. *What a difference a few hours make!* I walked into his office a loser, a quitter. After thanking him profusely and shaking his hand with the strength of The Incredible

Hulk, I walk out with a plan for success that will build on my strengths. *I am not leaving this University; I have a new and exciting program to finish!*

⁂

The coursework is challenging but exhilarating. I keep up with my organized study plan in classes where the students, including me, are talented and motivated. I am no longer a fish out of water, although I am the oldest student in the undergrad program. Reminding myself that age does not matter, I keep swimming.

⁂

Graduation day is here! I did it! Mr. Wonderful has a room reserved at a nearby restaurant for us to celebrate over lunch after the ceremony. My mother and sisters, his mother and Jim are all coming. The mood in our house is festive; everyone is busy getting ready. My sisters are all dressed up, touching up their makeup before we leave. My mother wears a new dress, and she looks beautiful. It's nice to see her smile and be part of this glorious day.

Mr. Wonderful needs to run to his office before heading to Commencement, and Jim will join us at the venue. He works just down the street and left early this morning to finish up a couple of things before taking the afternoon off. My baby sister, Louise, offers to drive the rest of us downtown. I am so nervous that me driving is not a good idea. We plan on arriving early, giving my sisters and mother plenty of time to save seats and get everyone to the right place. We are giggling on the way to the event, adding to my excitement! They drop me off in front of the building on their way to the parking garage. Before I shut the car door, Louise yells out, "See you soon, college graduate!" I love the sound of that!

⁂

The venue is enormous, with a capacity for thousands of people. There are quite a few families already here, and I see signs of congratulations for the graduates—chairs for the soon-to-be graduates line the floor. My heart stops for a moment. The aisle we will soon process down goes on forever.

Slowly, I turn, compose myself and head for my program's undergrad section. As I make my way down along the hallway, I see a group wearing gowns that differ from mine. A sign posted on the wall, Master's Program, tells me these are graduate students. To my right, another large room is filled with people wearing yet another type of gown, with velvet stripes on the sleeves. Their caps are different, and they are holding long, folded robes. The identifying sign, Doctoral Program, hangs on the door. *Wow, these students are graduating as doctors today.* I think momentarily about my dream, but I quickly get myself back in gear. I am here. I have accomplished my goal, and I will enjoy the entire day—first, the ceremony. Then onto lunch with family – truly a dream come true!

I find my group and see that, like me, everyone is smiling. Some women fix their makeup and hold mirrors to make sure their hair looks good under their mortarboards. It seems that I am not the only one worried about falling on the stairs. It turns into a big topic of conversation. An overhead announcement breaks through the chatter. "Congratulations, graduates. Please line up, as we will soon begin to proceed to the stage. Smile, and enjoy your Commencement Ceremony."

With military precision, we line up in our assigned order. Nervous giggles break out as we make our way to our seats. I remind myself to smile and look for my family, who plan on sitting to my left as I enter the arena. As we get closer to the auditorium, we can hear the song "Pomp and Circumstance" playing, and my heart skips a beat.

Walking in, we are greeted by families waving signs of well wishes, acknowledgments, and congratulations. But it is a sea of expectant faces, too many to pick out individual family members. I look down. I do not want to trip and make a spectacle of myself.

Commencement begins. The speakers are encouraging, inspiring, and exciting, and when remarks conclude, ushers direct the graduates to the stage, row by row. I take a moment to look around, and I am still unable to find any familiar faces.

An usher signals that it is time for our row to rise and walk down the aisle. Smoothing my gown, I begin to move toward the stage. Right, left, right, left, focus on walking. *Don't trip! Smile and enjoy this day!* But listening to the announcement of each graduate's name as they proceed across the stage, I find myself fighting back the tears—tears of joy.

The student ahead of me is already walking across the stage. I hear my name and begin walking right behind them.. Right, left, right, left. The President of the University extends his hand and smiles. "Congratulations!" He is looking straight at me! I can't hold back; the tears flow as I move to the other end of the stage. *Just three more little stairs, and you will be safely back in your seat.*

"Stop, hold it, smile!" A photographer politely asks me to pose for a photo before I continue down the aisle. Right, left, right, left. *Whew, you did it!* Back to the safety of my chair. No missteps, no falls, no embarrassing moments. I wipe my eyes with a tissue I strategically placed in my sleeve.

The President of the University gives his final thoughts and concludes by congratulating all of us on our accomplishments. We rise from our seats en masse and begin to make our way back to the staging area through waves of thunderous applause that continues as we exit and receive the signal to disperse. We move out quickly. We all want to get to our families. Walking up the stairs, I can not contain my excitement. I am now a college graduate, and my family is here to help me celebrate!

Lunch is a blur. Everyone shares their favorite part of the ceremony and how they were all trying to get my attention as I walked to the stage. There is so much joy in this room. Our waitress carries in a vase filled with a beautiful bouquet of roses and places it in the center of our table—a lovely gift from Jim. With a huge smile on her face, my mother hands me a small package that reveals a beautiful pen and pencil set when unwrapped.

As I thank everyone for coming and their generous presents, Mr. Wonderful announces that there is one more gift. He hands me a small envelope with a note inside that details our upcoming trip to New York City. We are leaving on the train tomorrow and staying for three days. He smilingly tells me that he bought tickets to the *Steel Magnolias* show on Broadway. Everyone laughs. They know it probably was not his first choice of shows. It was pure thoughtfulness for me. I am overwhelmed, jumping up to hug him and then walking around the table to hug everyone. I am not the only one crying. It feels so lovely to be able to celebrate and spend time in joy and happiness with those I love. I want this moment to go on forever.

MY LIFE'S PURPOSE

Following graduation, life took on a cadence, one of familiarity, routine, and prosperity. My sales career continued to go well. I loved the products I sold, the clinicians, colleagues, and managers with whom I worked. Mr. Wonderful and I were doing well financially, which allowed us the ability and time to travel and enjoy life. I was grateful for the life I had. And yet, I felt restless, called to explore what I was meant to do with my life. Instinctively, I knew that meant exploring health and wellness. I knew that meant becoming a practitioner.

I've always put my son's and husband's needs first, especially financially. Now I am determined to put myself first and follow my heart. Mr. Wonderful and I often discuss my desire to shift my career. "First, you wanted to go to college," he sighs, "and you did that. Now you want to change your career. What is next? When will you be happy?"

Once again, I find myself explaining, "I put my life on hold to raise my son, and I put your goals and desires ahead of mine. I never question your new endeavors or ideas to expand your business. Why can't you support me in mine?" I am a significant contributor to the financial health of our marriage, and Mr. Wonderful is obviously displeased with any pending change in that. Our conversations always end with the promise that we will discuss it later. Well, for me, later is now.

I begin to explore programs that would support my goal of shifting from medical sales representative to practitioner. Nursing was the obvious place to begin. After doing cursory research, I realized that I would need to start over academically. My undergraduate degree did not include enough science credits for admission to a nursing program. I continue my search. I am confident that I will find a program that will support my passion as a life-long learner and my desire to become a practitioner.

It is a rainy, chilly Saturday morning in March. I could not sleep last night, and I have been up for hours. Mr. Wonderful has an early appointment. He is getting ready to leave and will be gone most of the day. Drinking my coffee, I sit at my computer, scrolling through search results for healthcare practitioner and consultant programs. There it is! I click on the screen and begin reading about a local university offering graduate academic programs for acupuncture and herbal medicine. I jump to their website and start exploring. There is an informational open house … today! I jump into the shower, get dressed in record time, and head for my car. As I pull into the university parking lot, I no longer care about the bitter cold and driving rain.

I am greeted at the door and directed to help myself to a warm cup of tea and a name tag. With those in hand, I head toward the back of the room to find a seat. Several alumni take turns speaking to the audience about their academic experiences. I can not believe my ears! Many of them were career changers ... just like me! I find it challenging to stay in my seat! During the breakout sessions, I realize that the herbal medicine program is a perfect fit. As the open house comes to a close, I make a beeline to the admissions table. "I would like to talk with you about the application process." *This is it!*

Back home at my desk, I waste no time filling out forms, requesting transcripts, and gathering the information required for my admission. I find I can barely think, much less craft a cohesive letter of intent.

Mr. Wonderful arrives home. Almost dinner time, and I throw something together. A lot has happened on this dreary Saturday. I have spent the entire day tending to exciting plans for my new life— my next journey. Now, I just have to bring Mr. Wonderful up to speed.

I decide that I am not going to ask. I am going to state my desire to move forward with an application to this graduate program. It is a full-time, rigorous three-year program at an accredited university. I will need to quit my job. I have already made a rough draft of my plan, and have it all written down on paper. I decide I will share it with Mr. Wonderful over dinner.

Worst meal ever. Mr. Wonderful's response is less than wonderful. "I think you are selfish, asking me to support us while you lollygag at school. What is the point of another program? Just how many degrees do you want?"

I won't let him spoil my excitement. "I know this is a lot of information. But, if I am to acquire the knowledge necessary to become a practitioner, I need this academic program. Yes, finances will be tight for a while. This is something I want to do, and it will extend my career. Once I complete the program, I will contribute financially again."

With some finesse, I steer the conversation toward an agreement to have another talk after I learn the status of my application. Mr. Wonderful uses the words "if you get in" at the same time I say, "when I get in." I know I am right. And this time, I am not backing down!

Rushing through the dishes, I quickly get back to my desk. Lots of paperwork still to do. Noticing that I am gleefully returning to my desk to do paperwork on a Saturday night makes me smile!

It takes a couple of months for me to receive the news—my acceptance letter! The herbal medicine graduate program begins in September, just four months away. I am thrilled; Mr. Wonderful is most definitely not!

He is adamant that I maintain my sales job while working through the program. I do my best to convince him that I can not be in the classroom five days a week and still keep my full-time job. I want to hear him say that he believes in me, that he will support my dream. I do that for him, always willing to help him. I accuse him of seeing me as a 'paycheck with pants.' His growing concern about my continued significant contribution to our lifestyle is worrisome to me. I want to yell, scream, beg. I am growing tired, tired of having to explain and justify myself. *What am I going to do?*

It is three o'clock in the morning, and I can't sleep. I am completely miserable. In just a couple of hours, I will head to the airport ... again ... for another business trip. No matter how often I express my desire to quit my job, it falls on deaf ears. Last night, yet another argument about Mr. Wonderful's refusal to accept the fact that I can extend my career, and my contributions to our finances, by completing this master's program, not to mention the sheer joy of being able to become a practitioner. I also made it clear that I am miserable, that I want this chance, and that I wish I had a partner who supported my dreams. With his impatience growing, he headed for the door, saying, "I supported your decision to get your other undergraduate degree. What more do you want?"

I could not believe my ears and immediately snapped back, "I want the same consideration that I give you. When you tell me about your new ideas, I am right there to support you—not once have I asked how much it would cost. When you tell me about your golf trips with your buddies or a new business venture, I wish you well. I want you to trust that I won't take advantage of you, won't endanger our financial security. Of all people, I would hope that you know that!"

He slammed the door and left the house. I did not notice what time he got home. I slept in the spare bedroom, having no desire to spend any time with him right now. My bag is packed for my flight. I have been crying for hours. My eyes are swollen. My stomach is in knots. I want to scream and break things. I can't ever remember feeling this out of control, feeling like I am having a complete melt-down.

It is now five o'clock in the morning and almost time for me to leave. Mr. Wonderful stirs, peeks his head into the room, and asks if I want coffee. I see he is still planning to drive me to the airport. I want to scream but do my best to keep my voice level. Speaking through clenched teeth, I tell him, "I have decided to drive myself today. I do not want to spend any time with you before my flight.

Just go back to bed." He looks at me, puzzled. "Well, if that is what you want, have a nice flight," he says over his shoulder as he heads back to bed.

Have a nice flight? What a jerk! Carla, how did you get here…again! I am a nervous flier, petrified of planes. I have had this fear all my life, but I have been pushing through, flight after flight, to keep this job and bring in money. Telling me to 'have a nice flight' is such a passive-aggressive statement. I can't believe my ears.

I dress in record time, slamming every drawer and every door in the house. I want to make so much noise that Mr. Wonderful won't be able to sleep. Storming out of the house, I slam my car door and rev the engine as I squeal out of the driveway. I am crying so hard I can barely see. My hands are shaking as I concentrate on keeping the car on the road. I feel so incredibly alone. No one understands me. I spend my life taking care of everyone else, and when I get the nerve to ask for what I want, the answer is 'no.' *Why does it always have to be 'no'?*

Pulling into my space in the long-term parking lot, I glance in the mirror. I look pathetic—my face is red and swollen like I've just finished a few rounds in a prizefight. *This is ridiculous … You are a grown woman! What are you waiting for? Enough is enough. You are not living your life—you are just observing it. Do something about that!* I shove the key back into the ignition and head home. I know that by missing this upcoming flight, this upcoming meeting, I will be terminated. At this moment, I do not care. I need to do this. For me. For my life.

Walking in the door, I see Mr. Wonderful, dressed and on the phone. He looks shocked and quickly ends the call. I can't get the words out fast enough. My brain is close to malfunctioning; I stammer, "I can not do this anymore. I can't keep flying and going on trips. I can not keep denying my desire to change my career. I thought you would be part of my life, and I am fine if you do not want to do that anymore. I am quitting my job today, just as soon as I can catch my breath. If you want to end our marriage, then so be it!"

I get it all out and collapse on the sofa. I have been awake for more than twenty-four hours, pondering this decision. Still shaking, I do my best to compose myself. I am praying Mr. Wonderful will come over and give me a big hug, tell me it is all going to be alright, that he believes in me, in us. He does none of this. "Well," he says, as he gathers his briefcase and keys, "I guess we will figure this out." With that, he walks out the door.

I shower again and get dressed again. I call my manager, leaving a message that I missed my flight, and asking her to contact me. She calls me during a break in the meeting I was supposed to be attending, concerned about my absence. I briefly explain that I need to shift my priorities and that attending a full-time academic program requires my resignation from this sales job.

We go on to have a lovely conversation. She is incredibly understanding. "Once I am back home, we will talk next week about your plans to leave—no need to make this public yet. Until then, are you willing to continue working?" I assure her that I am, that I am in no hurry to leave, that my program does not start until September. "Great! We have plenty of time to make this work." With that, she heads back into her meeting.

Exhausted, I fall into bed and sleep until dinnertime. Today, I put myself first.

THE INFLUENCE OF TRADITIONAL MEDICINE

Singing along to the music blasting from my radio on a beautiful September morning, I am heading down the road toward another first day of school. This time I am starting as a graduate student in the Herbal Medicine Program. For the next three years, I will be learning about herbal medicine – its history and its impact on contemporary science and western medicine. The classes will be challenging, and the schedule looks to be grueling. The program requires us to attend all-day courses, five days a week, and a few weekends. As usual, I can barely contain my excitement about being back in the classroom. The campus is beautiful and includes plenty of outdoor green space, including a gorgeous herbal garden. I can see that I will enjoy every minute of my time in the magical place.

I am thrilled to be part of a small group of twenty students, and, after introductions, we realize we come from a variety of academic and career backgrounds. Each of us tells the group what brought us to this campus, to this program. The reasons are as varied as our experiences. What we have in common is our desire to succeed in our studies. I realize that in addition to the opportunity to become a practitioner, I am drawn to this program's traditional perspective on medicine, illness, and health.

The trimester covers plant physiology and pathophysiology, along with courses focused on all aspects of botanical medicine. We spend a great deal of time studying each plant, constituent, origins, actions, potential interactions, science data, and research. I make flashcards to help make an exhausting level of memorization possible.

In addition to academic work, classes focus on introspective and observational skills related to our individual health. We are encouraged to incorporate herbs into our daily lives, keeping notes on how they influence us. Combining clinical observation skills and the nature of botanical medicine is an essential part of the program. Because the course load is heavy, most of my class participates in study groups to ensure we keep up with the increasing volume of information and assignments. Through this process, we become close friends, sharing our experiences and the outcomes of our herbal experiments.

I plan to begin experimenting with herbal tea blends, syrups, and tinctures. Tinctures, which are herbs steeped in alcohol or vinegar, can be stored for long periods and taken in doses, measured in drops or teaspoons, as needed; syrups are made by boiling water and herbs, which shifts the texture and concentrates the flavor. Adding honey preserves the syrup, making shelf life longer. I choose to make elderberry syrup, a delicious option to boost the immune system. It is now one of my favorites. On cold winter mornings, I love a few drops in my tea!

I find this part of the course fascinating and extremely helpful. I am steeping myself in the traditional wisdom and knowledge of plant medicine that has been used for centuries, dating back to Hippocrates. Plants become magical for me as I learn about their phytochemical constituents such as saponins, tannins, phenols, bitters, and flavonoids. Even more intriguing to me is information on the actions of plants such as nervines, adaptogens, carminatives, bitters, expectorants, and tonics, just to name a few. It is a whole new world of knowledge opening up and presenting a completely different view of the power of herbal plants, the healing power of medicinal herbal plants.

A keen area of interest for me is studying the history of researchers who isolated plant components in order to create medicines. While I began my courses with a basic understanding that, over the years, plants and herbs inspired researchers and scientists to investigate the mechanisms of plant action to create synthetic drugs, I had no idea how all of this had evolved. For example, I am amazed to learn that willow bark was used by many cultures to calm inflammation and reduce fever for many thousands of years. Over time, scientists isolated an active ingredient, salicin, and used that to treat fever. This led to the manufactured drug aspirin dating back to the 1800s. Following the creation of aspirin and the development of so many other pharmaceuticals, the beauty and influence of botanical medicine seem to have waned in clinical importance for many physicians. As for me, I understand the herbalists' passion and drive to elevate herbal medicine in contemporary relevance. For many, herbal medicine can have the same impact, perhaps a more profound impact on a person's health than manufactured drugs.

I begin to understand the significant impact on my mother from taking so many medications over the years, primarily because the side effects she had from one pill resulted in her physician prescribing another medication. As the daughter of a woman who did not receive proper treatment, I also realize that I have also been significantly impacted by the effect of multiple medications on my mother's life and health. I wonder how this information might have positively shaped the trajectory of my mother's overall health and wellness.

I want to design a practice where I can work with people who want to learn how to support their health. I desire to become part of a movement that goes beyond fixing symptoms. I want to initiate conversations grounded in the information I am learning in my classes. Information that has opened my eyes to the significance of behavior change and the impact those changes can have on overall wellbeing. Thankfully, I am in an academic program that supports this view and will enable me to graduate with the credentials needed to really help people, not just rely on prescriptions.

I begin to seriously focus on my own health. I have struggled with migraines my entire life. By investigating the impact of stress, and the influence of food, sleep, and exercise, I consider how I might change some things in my life that could positively impact my wellbeing. By shifting to whole-food dietary choices, focusing on hydration, mindfulness, and continuing physical movement, my body may be able to transition toward healing.

I research herbs that support the alleviation of chronic stress, allow me to relax, and mitigate headaches. I choose several that I find most interesting, including lavender, passionflower, chamomile, and ashwagandha. It is a fantastic revelation for me: by concentrating on the root causes of my headaches, rather than clearing the pain of my migraines, I can finally see results. In many instances, I identify the symptoms and minimize the impact, severity, and recurrences of my headaches. These observations propel me to research other herbs, and my experiments continue to yield illuminating results: less frequent sinus congestion, better sleep through the reduction of stress. Herbs are, indeed, powerful medicine!

Time passes quickly as fall turns to winter and then, seemingly immediately, to spring. Typically, summer means time off from classes. But my classmates and I are in a full-time program—no break for us. We make the best of it by spending a great deal of time outside. Some of our professors even give their lectures outdoors, a fantastic treat!

I can not hide my excitement about being in this program, and I make no effort to do so. Mr. Wonderful tolerates some discussion about my classes but quickly loses interest. He rolls his eyes when I mention that I need to do homework on weekends. His hypocrisy puzzles me. I remind him that his job requires him to work most weekends, but I do not complain. At times, I feel sad that he is not more enthusiastic and supportive. He is supposed to be my best friend. My classmates often share how their significant others made dinner, helped them study for an exam, or brought flowers at the end of a difficult semester. Green with envy, I smile and tell them how great it is to have such wonderfully supportive partners. They do not need to know that I am not personally experiencing these gestures. I will keep that to myself.

Without much support in my home, I continue to immerse myself in my studies. The magic inspires me to research a topic and discover new facts, ideas, and points of view. Often it is challenging, sometimes frustrating, and at times overwhelming. And yet, I feel called to continue moving forward. My primary motivation is not or has not been the acquisition of a degree. My driver is the continued process of learning something new, up-leveling my skill set, and cultivating new skills by acquiring knowledge, based on the work of those I admire and aspire to be. I love learning, delving into ideas and data that offer new ideas, perspectives, and possibilities! I recall my elementary school book report about the country's first female physician, Dr. Elizabeth Blackwell, and realize that I am closer to my dream of becoming a practitioner myself.

School is going well, and my first year has wrapped. My second and final year of classes begins in September. In twelve short months, I will take a final exam and hopefully move into the program's clinical practice, where I will see clients under the direction and supervision of clinical staff—the clinic portion of the program shifts from classroom activities to clinical skills and practitioner training. In just one year, I will move out of the classroom and into the university's clinic treatment rooms, helping clients by utilizing what I have learned! I become a bit nervous when I think about it, but the ability to practice herbal medicine to support my patients' health is beyond exciting.

Life at home is a continual strain. To avoid having to deal with his heavy sighs and elaborate eye rolls, I hide my schoolbooks when Mr. Wonderful is due to come home from his office. To avoid irritating him, I have stopped sharing interesting tidbits I learn in class. I do most of my studying at my desk, out of sight, or when he is away at appointments. This seems to minimize the friction: out of sight, out of mind. I remain optimistic that Mr. Wonderful will soon see my joy, understand my commitment, and recognize my new career's potential ahead of me. The truth is, I want him to be happy for me, feel proud of me, and support my new endeavor.

Time quickly passes, and the workload continues to intensify. Many of us struggle to keep up and worry about the upcoming exam at the end of November. Thankfully, after the exam, we will have a significant break in December, which helps to keep us going.

My favorite classes focus on clinical skills: interviewing techniques, physical assessment, and creating clinical recommendation plans. I throw myself into my studies and continue to do well, even though a few exams have taught me to be humble. My test anxiety dogs me in this program just as it has in every academic course I have ever taken. I get upset when I know I have studied well but receive a less-than-ideal grade after taking an exam. This seems to manifest most in math and science classes. No matter how prepared I am prior to sitting down to take quizzes, tests, or exams, my anxiety to do well takes over, and my brain freezes. I make an effort to remain mindful and to keep breathing, not letting negative thoughts take over. I do my best to keep it under control, and I struggle with it in every class.

As I progress through this program, however, my confidence continues to build. I immerse myself by participating in my study group, cementing complex concepts into understandable – and memorable – content. Because the material interests me, I find test-taking easier now than at any time in my academic career.

My hard work pays off. I pass my comprehensive exams and will be heading off to the clinic in January! I have completed the classroom portion of the program, and I will soon transition to student practitioner! I am just as thrilled to learn that Mr. Wonderful and I will celebrate my successful completion of the exam by going out to dinner. The dinner is his idea! He selects the restaurant, makes the reservations, and brings home a beautiful bouquet before leaving the house.

Over a glass of wine, he apologizes for his emotional distance these last few months, sharing that work has been challenging. He is looking forward to enjoying some time off, as am I. We talk about the upcoming holidays and make plans to spend time together. I feel so much joy I can barely sit still. My best friend, Mr. Wonderful, is back in my corner. I am more deeply in love with him than I thought possible. My husband, my best friend, is happily supporting me. We both decide that this will be the best holiday ever! Dinner is filled with joyous laughter, his wicked wit front and center. The tension is gone. The mood is light and cheerful, brimming with contentment. *So, this is what support feels like...this is what my classmates have described! It feels terrific, and I can not wait to see what the future brings.*

DECEMBER 28TH

The holidays this year are delightful. We are having a pleasant time with family and each other. I spend time thinking about how grateful I am that Mr. Wonderful has done an about-face from his objection to me working towards my degree in herbal medicine rather than working in medical sales. His support of my academic goals are precious to me. I decide to make a nice dinner, so Mr. Wonderful and I can sit down together when he gets home.

Dinner is almost ready when he walks in the door. We chat and eat and, after cleaning up the dishes together, settle in for a quiet evening watching a movie. In short order, Mr. Wonderful's cell phone rings. Lately, he is always busy with work. He glances at the phone and then says he just remembered that he needs to pick something up from the mall.

"It is 8:30 at night," I said, "You may not make it before the mall closes. Can't it wait until tomorrow?" He is changing sweaters and pulling on his boots. "The mall is open later for the holidays. I won't be too long."

As the door closes behind, I begin to feel a strange sensation in the pit of my stomach. The mall? At this hour? *He feels* the need to go to the mall after *a phone call?* I hear the car pull away and realize that my heart is beating faster. What *is* he up to? The voice of reason in my head wonders why I doubt my husband. *Are you just looking for a reason to be upset? Maybe he is getting you a post-Christmas gift.* Telling myself I am making something out of nothing, I make a concerted effort just to let it go.

Later, loading the dishwasher, I glance at the clock on the wall. It is now almost 9:30. Something is just not right. As my gut heaves again, I go into detective mode. I start in his office, looking through the papers scattered across his desk. I look at his emails. Nothing seems suspicious – just work-related messages. *Whew…just my imagination.* I feel bad about doubting him, but something is bugging me – this nagging voice telling me to stick with it … to dig deeper. Before getting up, I go through his emails more carefully, this time searching his sent messages folder.

As I scroll, I ask myself what I am doing and decide to stop. Just as I am reaching to close the laptop, a message leaps out at me. It is addressed to someone I don't know, a woman whose name I do not recognize. Mr. Wonderful's message reminds her to be sure to pack her passport for their trip to Canada in February. Canada? In February? We have a timeshare in Canada; is he taking *her* there? I click on the message and nervously read through it. He goes on to say how excited he is to be going skiing with her in a few short weeks. I stop breathing and re-read the email. Again, and again, and again.

Scrolling further, I find a message from a luxury hotel asking for feedback on a recent stay. I can't believe what I am seeing. *Is this a joke?* My best friend, my Mr. Wonderful, stayed in a luxury hotel and has plans to take another woman to our timeshare. My gut is in knots, and I am dangerously close to throwing up. My hands are sweaty and shaking. I am numb. *How is this possible? How did this happen?* My Mr. Wonderful is having an affair.

Sitting at his desk, I am unable to move. I feel like I am in a fog. I decide to print the emails. One side of my brain tells me that this gives me the chance to re-read them to make sure I have the facts straight. The other side of my brain tells me I will need them as proof if Mr. Wonderful decides to delete them later. I need to be practical, always practical. And I have had a lifetime of practice being practical.

After a few moments, a plan forms in my head, and I push myself into execution. I pack an overnight bag and put it in my car. I go back to the kitchen and make a cup of tea – something to calm my nerves as I mull over my next move. And then I wait.

After what feels like hours, he finally returns home, smiling and in a good mood. He just bought a sweater that he has had his eye on and decided to treat himself, happy that it was still available and happier yet that it was on sale.

I return his smile and agree that his purchase is wonderful. "Hey, I have been thinking," I am no longer interested in talking about the stupid sweater. "I know I said I couldn't go skiing with you in February because of school, but I think I can make it work now. I looked over my course calendar and, if I make arrangements with my professors, I can turn in my assignments early so I can go to the timeshare with you. I wanted to surprise you; isn't that great!"

His face turns white. I mean, like the color of a kindergarten paste. "I know you hate to fly," he stammers, "and I thought I would ask one of the guys to go so that we can just relax and ski."

I want to believe him. I try to forget the emails I had just read. I want life to go back to what it was yesterday, the way it was before he left to go to the mall tonight. And yet, I suddenly realize that yesterday was not what I thought it was. He had a girlfriend yesterday and for many months before that. My life, as I know it, is over.

Speaking around a massive knot in my throat, not sure I will be able to talk, I know I have to ask. I have to know the answer. "What about your girlfriend? Will she want to be part of your guy trip? Does she like to ski?"

He is visibly shaken and getting angry at my questions. "What are you talking about? Have you lost your mind?" I look deep into his eyes. He is convincing, but... "I know the truth!" I shriek. I can't hold back any longer. Tears are streaming down my face, and my mind is racing. His continuous denials are sickening. He is lying to my face, acting as if I have lost my mind. Enough is enough. I walk through the front door, get in my car, and speed out of the driveway. I just need to get to the nearest hotel without causing an accident.

Thankfully, the hotel lobby is relatively empty. It is nearly 11 o'clock now as I approach the front desk and ask for a room. "Are you alright, ma'am? How can I help you?"

I quickly realize that I must look like a mess, my red eyes and tear-streaked pasty face a testament to the complete implosion of my life. "Can I check into this hotel without putting my name on the room registry? I need to get away from my husband. I want to feel safe, but I am worried he may be looking for me." The desk clerk assures me that they don't give out personal information. Just to be sure, I use the name Jane Smith. I am not sure Mr. Wonderful is even concerned enough to look for me. Even so, I do not want to be found. I need to be alone. I need to find a minute of peace.

I am emotionally exhausted, hurt, angry, and scared. For the first time in my life, I completely trusted someone. I have been working and basically supporting myself since I was seventeen, and now, because I quit my job to attend school, I have absolutely no income. Mr. Wonderful is moving on with his life – WITHOUT ME! My head pounding, my gut twisted like a pretzel, I crawl into bed and begin to sob.

The beginning of a new day shines through the drapes. It is still really early, but I am wide awake. As I lie in bed thinking about what happened last night, I feel completely empty. Sadness seems to ooze from my pores. I need to eat something. Hoping that a hot breakfast will help me feel better, I order room service. After just two bites, I decided to put my breakfast in the small refrigerator with plans to reheat it later. I decide that perhaps a walk would help to ease my mind.

Stepping off the elevator, I stare at a magnificently decorated Christmas tree prominently displayed in the lobby. I want to fall to the floor, melt into a puddle. I had not noticed it when I checked into the hotel last night. Keeping a stiff upper lip, I smile at the front desk staff and act like I forgot something, requiring me to go back to my room. I quickly press the button and hope the elevator arrives quickly, as I feel the tears just beginning to make their presence.

Thankfully, the elevator opens, and it is empty. I make my way to the room and climb back into bed. Day turns into night and back into day. I sleep through it all.

The following two days are a blur. I turn on my cell phone periodically and listen to Mr. Wonderful's messages. All of them. "Are you okay? I'm worried about you. Please call to tell me you are okay." Including this, "Yes, you were right – I am having an affair. Please come home so we can talk about it." I already know I am right. I have read the emails a couple of hundred times since I left home.

On the morning of the third day, I decide it is time to go home. Actually, the decision was made for me as my room is no longer available. The hotel is booked solid, preparing for the arrival of the New Year's Eve crowd. Somewhere, people are getting ready to celebrate the promise of a new year. Oh, how I wish I could join them.

ACTING AS IF I KNOW WHAT I AM DOING

January, usually a month for setting visionary goals and planning how to achieve them, finds me barely able to get out of bed. So many failed marriages. I feel entirely alone and abandoned. In addition to the isolation, I am terrified about my future. I trusted Mr. Wonderful with both my emotional and my financial life. Now I need to take care of myself – emotionally and financially. I feel unable to do either. How did I get this so wrong?

Mr. Wonderful has moved out. He says he will find a place to rent, says I can stay in our family home until we can make other arrangements. *Other arrangements?* Not two weeks ago, we were enjoying a festive meal, drinking wine, and celebrating the holidays. Now he tells me that we need to decide how to move forward. *Move forward?* Our conversations cease.

I am wary of sharing the news, the news of yet another failed relationship. Jim needs to be the first person I tell. I want him to hear directly from me. But he is enjoying a brief holiday vacation with his dad, and I don't want to cause him any distress. I also do not want to share any details. I want Jim's focus to remain on his own life, not on me and another colossal blunder. I still feel tremendous guilt about the mistakes I made in parenting him. I was a young mother who really learned on the job, with minimal support and no real role model. I wish that I could spare Jim from hearing this news. I decide to call him and tell him that Mr. Wonderful and I are just separating. There will be time for the ugly truth and details later.

As for Mr. Wonderful, he is still reeling from guilt. He assures me that he will take care of my monthly household bills until I finish my program, including making the mortgage payments so I can stay in the house. I feel a sense of relief, at least for now.

A good friend and work colleague, Taylor, calls to check in on me. She heard the news and wants to share her story of painful betrayal, which is eerily similar to mine. "I don't want to cause you any more pain, and I pray that you won't experience what I went through, but I want you to be prepared." Taylor went on, "In my case, my husband's guilt lasted about sixty days. In no time at all, the guilt was gone, and he served me with divorce papers." Before I can protest, Taylor continues, "he will find ways to blame you for the breakup. And he won't honor his commitment to take care of you financially, especially with a new girlfriend as his new priority. Do not let your guard down."

I am stunned, and yet I know in my gut that my friend's warning is sound. I need to be prepared for a sudden change of heart by Mr. Wonderful. After all, he just proved that he could change his mind. My best friend, my partner, my Mr. Wonderful just threw me away – threw us away. I want my experience to be different than Taylor's. I want to believe that he will honor his word—this time.

It turns out I am surprised again. After a couple of months, Mr. Wonderful begins to express his displeasure with me, my career aspirations, and my academic program – which he says is draining his finances. He is angry about having to pay for a mortgage and rent. He does not feel it is fair that he is expected to support me while I go to school—while I am not working and contributing financially. Taylor's advice to be prepared was well-founded; her prediction that guilt does not last very long was prophetic.

Thanks to social media, I learn about his new circle of friends – with his now girlfriend. She went from mistress to girlfriend in a flash. They are having a blast! As they attend party after party, I sink deeper into depression, spending my days in the house, closed off from the world. I do my best to find ways to occupy my mind. Reading, which I usually enjoy, is now a chore. It is hard to concentrate. I turn on the television, choosing home improvement and cooking shows over romantic comedies, which are just too much to bear. The sound of the television in the background breaks up the silent isolation of being alone in the house. I realize that if I am going to get through this, I have to push myself to connect with my friends. So, I gather up my courage and head toward the phone, calling a friend, Darcy, to ask her and her husband, Ron, over for dinner. I love to cook, and having guests enjoy a meal together lifts my spirits. This will be an enjoyable way to ease into becoming social again. I muster all the courage I have and begin dialing their number.

Darcy does not immediately speak after hearing my invitation. I sense that she is uncomfortable and is having difficulty responding. Clearing her throat, she says, "I am sorry. We already have plans." A pause. "I want to be honest with you and not have you find out from someone else. We have been invited over to Mr. Wonderful's house – he is hosting a dinner party. We have accepted and are planning to go."

I try my best to sound inquisitive rather than hostile. "I am a bit surprised that you want to socialize with him and his new mistress, after what he just did to me. How could you sit and have a meal with them? I feel tears welling up, and there is a knot in my throat. After another pause, she answers, "Carla, we don't want to get in the middle of this. And we certainly don't want to choose sides. This is awkward. I am sorry."

Awkward? She is sorry? She doesn't want to choose sides? Well, she just did! I feel myself melting into the floor. "I have to tell you that I am disappointed. If the situation were reversed, I would have no trouble choosing sides. I would be on your side after such a betrayal." She says that she will call me next week and I hang up. I know that our friendship is over. At least it is for me.

I never expected to have to prepare myself for this type of situation. Over the following weeks, very few of my other friends call or reach out. *Am I the one who did something wrong? Do my friends think I have brought this on myself?* I begin to feel as if everyone is leaving me. I understand that they may not know what to say, and ignoring me makes me feel worse.

I have some hard decisions to make. I may have to find a job to take care of myself. I can't believe I have to contemplate withdrawal from another academic program, which starts back up in a week. But I do not know if I can trust Mr. Wonderful to pay at least some of my bills so that I can finish this time. *How did I get here—again?* My fears overwhelm me—again. I feel as if I am walking through molasses, moving in a haze. The world has gone dark, and I am teetering on the edge of an abyss —nothing to look forward to, nothing to grab onto, nothing to do but fall in.

By the time classes resume, I have decided I will act "as if." As if nothing untoward has happened in my marriage. As if I have every confidence that I will finish my program with flying colors. As if my belief in myself has not been shattered. I pour every drop of my energy into acting "as if" in the hope that I will convince everyone —even myself.

Somehow, I will pull this off, and I will finish this program. I muster up the strength to smile at myself in the mirror as I walk out the front door. I am convinced I will hide all my pain and move forward. Once in the classroom, the energy is palpable. Everyone is excited and upbeat about our transition from classroom to clinic. The room is abuzz with those sharing stories about their activities over the holiday break. I act my heart out, delivering my update on the wonderful time spent with family and ending with how glad I am to be back. This is neither the time nor the place to share what really happened.

I have promised myself that while I am here, I will concentrate on school. There will be time to fall apart–again—at home. Home. Sadly, the word no longer holds meaning for me anymore. But I know if I focus on getting through this next year, on completing this program—I can focus on creating a new life for myself.

Time passes quickly. I continue to hide my pain as I move through the program, maintaining an optimistic demeanor. I immerse myself in honing my clinical skills and observational techniques and absorbing the research needed to create treatment plans for my clients. I find solace in knowing that I am making progress. Nothing will stop me from my goal. In less than a year, I will graduate with a master's degree in herbal medicine. Thankfully, my acting skills are paying off. No one is suspicious of my heartbreak or my over-whelming sense of fear and anxiety. I have become an award-winning actress. No one has any idea of what is going on behind my smile.

As I contemplate my next steps, I decide that it is time for me to move on, to take control of my life. I am tired of feeling sorry for myself. Every time I walk through the door, I am reminded of the tension in the house, the sleepless nights, the feelings of inadequacy and helplessness. I want to rid myself of memories of Mr. Wonderful. I no longer want to live in this house of betrayal and lies.

In no time, I find a new place to live and begin making plans to move. I will start over, and I will fill my new home with joy, happiness, and comfort.

I pick up my phone and begin dialing. "I need to talk with you about my plans for my future. I want to move out, and I need to find out about your financial plans to end this marriage." I am pleased with my tone and my ability to remain calm as I speak with Mr. Wonderful over the phone. What he shares sends me into another tailspin, another moment of utter disbelief. "I do not think it is fair for me to have to give you so much money. My business has had quite a few unexpected expenses, and I can't help you buy another home. I think I am paying enough now, taking care of your tuition and your living expenses. I think enough is enough."

Am I hearing him correctly? Enough is enough! Taylor's warning had been spot-on. Mr. Wonderful is concerned about his finances, about taking care of his new girlfriend! He is not honoring another promise made to me.

I decide to seek legal advice and make an appointment with an attorney. Leaving his office, I feel deflated. It is a jarring reminder that this is real. It is permanent, and it is all too familiar. I am angry that I am here again. I can barely contain the disdain I feel for myself. *How did I let this happen? Why am I continuing to bring sadness and heartbreak into my life? What on earth am I doing wrong?* The lawyer is quick to tell me that I have a case, that I could fight it out in court. "The only problem, my dear," he says kindly, leaning across his giant mahogany desk, "is that he can make this miserable for you. He can drag this out, and the only winners will be the attorneys. I wish I could tell you that he will do the honorable thing. Most men in these circumstances do. Sadly, some do not, and your husband appears to be one of those who are not honorable at all."

I leave his office and sit in my car, once again dissolving in tears. So much for my belief that he will do the right thing. Another betrayal. Mr. Wonderful's final betrayal. *Now what, Carla? Now what?*

The ringing phone interrupts my train of thought as I try to finish a clinical paper. Picking up, I immediately recognize the caller. "Hey, nice to hear your voice. I thought I would reach out and check in on you. I heard the news, and have to say I am shocked. Got a minute to talk?" A blast from the past. Mr. Personality.

I decide to take a break, and we have a pleasant conversation. I am guarded, sharing just enough to be friendly. My divorce from Mr. Personality was over eleven years ago. However, I am still embarrassed to be in this situation, with another marriage down the tubes and a financial bind keeping me awake at night. I won't share everything. It does feel nice to talk, and we share a few laughs. He asks if he can call again, and we agree to catch up the following week.

A few telephone conversations lead to a lunch outing. Walking into the restaurant, I am nervous, not sure what to expect. We chat briefly about the collapse of my marriage and the unintended impact on my bank account. Mr. Personality says he feels regret over the end of our relationship and his inability to understand how much school meant to me. He tells me that he feels differently now, that he sees that he made a big mistake in letting me go. He would like us to be friends. He is not in a relationship and would like to continue to see me.

I want to believe him, and I wonder what brought all of this on. *Why the sudden change?* Part of me is heartened by his interest in my plans to complete school and become a practitioner. And another big part is screaming at me. *Be careful!* I am conflicted. I want to trust him and believe his words. But past mistakes make me suspicious, unsure if I should—once again—ignore my gut, my instincts. Maybe he is sincere. Perhaps he has come to his senses, realizing that I was a great wife. I don't want to live the rest of my life wondering if I missed an opportunity. *What if this is real? What if this is our second chance to find love and happiness?* I decide to move forward with an open mind and a guarded heart.

We are enjoying spending time together. It is easy to be with him—familiar, fun, and enjoyable. He is attentive and shows interest in my life. When our families discover that we are spending time together, they encourage us to continue. Our relationship is moving toward commitment. On the one hand, I am nervous about this. It is happening so quickly. On the other hand, perhaps he really did miss me, miss us—and this was meant to be all along. I am pulled toward the familiar, wanting to be loved by someone who knows me. I know I am drawn to the idea of the family I have always wanted, the idea of someone having my back. I am tired of fighting so hard, tired of being alone and sad. I look at this as a new beginning, and, on blind faith, I move in with him.

The timing of the move is just before Christmas, and I settle in quickly. Our respective children and his grandchildren are pleased and enjoy a lovely holiday meal together, the house filled with laughter and joy. Seeing the little ones tear open their gifts brings back a flood of fond memories. It is lovely to have my Jim staying with us, visiting for the holidays. He tells us all about his place and job in New York City, and we excitedly plan a trip to see him after my graduation.

With the holidays wrapping up and our children back in their respective homes, it is time for me to focus on my program, which I will complete in a few short months. Mr. Personality and I have had many discussions about my herbal medicine program, and he appears to support my goals wholeheartedly. As always, the last weeks fly by, and before I know it, it is St. Patrick's Day—my last day in the clinic and, technically, my last day in school.

I meet with my advisor in the afternoon, making final preparations for my program's completion. Just a few signatures from my faculty supervisors and an audit of my charts, and I am done. In no time, I am jumping for joy. It's a wrap … I completed my graduate program! I call Mr. Personality to share my good news, telling him I am on my way home. In anticipation that everything would go well this afternoon, we make reservations for dinner. I can not contain my joy, smiling as I drive home. I can't wait to get home and share this excitement. I wonder what surprise Mr. Personality has waiting for me to celebrate this incredible milestone in our lives.

Walking in the door, I find Mr. Personality napping on the sofa. Part of me is stunned. *How can he sleep during such an exciting time?* I shrug it off, telling myself that, although this is my exciting day, he is just tired. He quickly wakes up, having heard me come in, and hugs me. "I just dozed off. More tired than I thought after work. Well, how do you feel?" Just as I start to answer, the phone rings. It is a business call for him, which of course, he answers. I head upstairs to get ready for dinner, feeling a bit disappointed. I thought the atmosphere at home would be more festive. I chastise myself once again. *Stop being dramatic. Let it go.*

❧

Jim arrives, holding the most exquisite orchid I have ever seen. "I thought I'd give this to you before we leave for the ceremony. It is really delicate, and it would not be good for it to be carried around all afternoon." It is so good to see him. Mr. Personality's children cannot attend today's ceremony due to other commitments, and I am looking forward to spending time and celebrating this moment with Jim.

The commencement ceremony is small and lovely, with thoughtful comments delivered by several speakers. I proudly introduce my son to many of my classmates—now colleagues—and chat about our favorite parts of the ceremony. In no time, it's over, and I head home. We say goodbye to Jim, whose train is leaving shortly. We plan to talk in the next few days about booking our trip to visit him in New York soon.

I watch Jim pull away and close the door. Mr. Personality tells me he is tired and ready to go to bed. *Go to bed? It's only eight o'clock!* I am still reveling in my excitement—my accomplishment. I am not ready to go to bed. I take off my gown and carefully fold it up, placing it next to my cap on a chair. I wash up, take off my makeup, and look in the mirror.

The lackluster end to my graduation day brings a hint of sadness to my face. I smile wryly at my reflection, silently congratulating myself on a job well done, and make my way to the kitchen. Alone with a hot cup of tea, I read the graduation cards I have received over the past few days. I just earned my master's degree, and I am sitting in this kitchen all alone. I just want to cry.

❧

Weeks later, I learn that Mr. Personality wasn't so excited about my going to school and is just glad it is over. He is looking forward to having an everyday life without having my attention focused elsewhere. Initially, I am stunned. But I soon revert to my routine and tell myself that I am overly sensitive. I just need to be grateful that I finished my program so I can move on. Once again, I ignore the big red flag flapping in front of my face. *It will get better. You just need to try harder. You need to try to be a better wife.*

COLORING OUTSIDE THE LINES

I am fast approaching my fiftieth birthday—a milestone. I want to do something significant, something just for me. Something I had never done before. Maybe something physical? I read an ad about a local triathlon scheduled for next August. On the surface, it does not seem to be the best choice for me. My swimming skills are self-taught, minimal at best. I am not an accomplished bicyclist or runner. Not sure why I convince myself that I have eight months to train. Eight months to become a participant in an Iron Girl Triathlon.

This particular triathlon is a top-rated event, and registration typically sells out within minutes after registration opens. I make it my mission to be at my computer and ready to register when the site goes live. In the middle of my training—in May—I turn fifty. Happy birthday to me!

My announcement that I have successfully entered the triathlon is met with quite a bit of skepticism. The support of my new goal is underwhelming, to say the least. I was hoping that Mr. Personality would be pleased and supportive. After all, I am not in school. How could my participation in a triathlon interfere with our family? At a holiday party, I mention to my good friend, Vanessa, my newly envisioned goal. Thankfully, Vanessa, who is always incredibly supportive, volunteers to help with my training. Vanessa is an accomplished athlete and was a competitive swimmer. She volunteers to help me prepare and recommends a training plan that starts with a goal of swimming at least once a week. We agree to join the local community pool and will meet every Friday morning, beginning in January.

This is my first morning. I promptly pull into the parking lot at 6:30 am. It is still dark outside. Vanessa parks right next to me and jumps out of her car. She is enthusiastically telling me how much fun this will be. I smile and nervously agree. It is January, it is freezing, and I am going swimming? What have I gotten myself into?

It is empty inside. The man at the front desk explains that we can purchase a day pass, a month pass, or a six-month pass. Vanessa wastes no time, "Six-month access pass for each of us, please. We are training for a triathlon." The minute he hands me the receipt, my stomach begins to churn. He directs us to the locker rooms, and, as we walk away, he smiles and calls out, "Have fun, ladies!" Hmmm. Fun indeed.

Vanessa and I quickly make our way down the hallway and lay claim to a locker. I don't want to take off my sweatshirt. It is beyond chilly in here. But I coax myself to push through. *You have made it this far. Get going!* The pool lanes are mostly empty. Go figure. Not too many crazy people at the pool at 6:45 on a frigid January morning. Vanessa suggests we share a lane so I can learn technique and form. *How is she able to be so happy, so enthusiastic? I am miserable, nervous, and wondering what the heck I am doing here!*

A splash, and I am in the water. *Good grief, it is cold* ... I thought this pool was heated! Feeling as if I just jumped into an ice cooler, Vanessa shouts and tells me to keep moving. "It will get warmer," she assures me. So, we begin to swim a few laps and then take a short break to chat. I let Vanessa do all the talking so I can catch my breath. I had no idea how hard this was going to be! The lanes seem to go on for miles.

After an hour, I am exhausted and beyond cold. Frustrated, I can not wait to get out of this pool and into a hot shower. As the water pounds on my back, I finally begin to feel warm again and head toward my locker. My fleecy sweatshirt is calling. I am still shivering as I put on my clothes. I turn toward Vanessa with a pathetic look on my face, and we begin to laugh. "It gets easier over time. We need to keep our focus on the goal of swimming in the race, not on the discomfort that we are feeling right now." Well, right now, I can't wait to get to my car and crank the heater to full blast. But Vanessa goes on, "Next, we will expand our schedule and start running right after we swim." *Good grief!*

Spring is here. Months of training pass, and it is now time to get out my bike and brush up on all the techniques for shifting gears. I have convinced myself that biking will be easier than running. But I want to give up after our first ride. My legs are on fire, and my butt is sore. "Don't worry, it gets easier," Vanessa says. Again, with the pep talk. "We will keep going until you feel comfortable." I can't help but deliver a snarky response. "Oh, so we are going to be at this until I celebrate my ninetieth birthday?" Vanessa laughingly reminds me that this was my idea. Of course, she is right. But who said it was a good idea?

Today's the day! It is five in the morning, and I am nervously getting dressed. I did not need the alarm this morning. My stomach has been in knots, and I pray my bowels don't get any funny ideas today. I hear Jim in the kitchen, grumbling about how early it is. I am so grateful that he was able to join me this weekend. Mr. Personality also expresses his displeasure that he is up so early on a Sunday morning, and this will all be over after today. "I am so tired of hearing about this triathlon," he grumbles—just another happy start to another day in our home.

❧

The day passes in a blur. The starting pistol fires, and I run to the water, jump in, and swim for what feels like miles and miles. Jumping out, I put on my gear, grab my bike, and hit the road. My legs are burning, they feel like jelly, and I am completely out of breath. Jim, Vanessa, and Mr. Personality are cheering me on from the stands. This helps to give me some energy as I pedal up a hill. Moving over to the slow lane allows the faster women to pass me, which is most of them. In no time, I have the road to myself. After sixteen grueling miles, I finally spot my pathway back into the park entrance. It is a most welcome sight. I coast down the hill and rack my bike. I take a big drink of water and begin the final leg of the triathlon—the run—which in my case, turns out to be a fast walk. Okay, a slow tortoise-like walk. My entire body aches. Even my eyelashes hurt. *Three miles, Carla, three more miles, and your triathlon is over! This torture will be over! Never again....never ever again!*

In the park, the atmosphere is festive. Music plays and cheering family members line the trails. Overhead, a speaker blares, announcing the names of runners as they cross the finish line. I can do this ... I am almost done. I see the sign marked that there is just one mile to the finish line. The end is near. Next to me, I see an older woman walking at the same pace. She tells me this is her fourth triathlon, and she has decided it will be her last. "I have accomplished my goal, and at age seventy-five, I want to try new things." Seventy-five! She has the most pleasant attitude and congratulates me on MY accomplishment. We both begin to pick up our pace just a bit. As we near the finish line, she looks over at me. "Okay, we just have a few feet to go. It is time to begin to pick up our pace. Let's jog!" We cross the finish line together, and, with the little bit of breath I have left, I thank her and wish her well.

The first person I see is Jim, running toward me. "You did it, Mother, you did it!" I can't hold back the tears. I can't breathe, and I am beyond exhausted. Thankfully, Jim hands me a bottle of cold water and then folds me into a hug. Mr. Personality half-heartedly congratulates me, saying, "I knew you could do it." Vanessa is jumping up and down and hands me a lovely bouquet. I begin to notice several other friends who have joined my 'cheering section.' Friends who are spending their Sunday afternoon watching me finish my race…completely heartwarming.

As we are chatting about my day's adventures, my friends invite us to join them for pizza. I know my son needs to get back to his home, but sitting down and enjoying a large, cheesy pizza sounds great. Before I can answer, though, Mr. Personality jumps in, "No, thanks anyway. I am sure Carla is tired and wants to rest. We have been here all day and have some things to do at home." After brief hugs and goodbyes, we all head in separate directions.

The ride home is quiet. I am too tired to find out why. *What could I have possibly done now?* Mr. Personality breaks his silence when we get home. "Go up and take your shower. I have to clean out the back of the truck. It is filthy. Your bike is full of sand and dirt and I need to go to the car wash and vacuum it out." *Really? Is that it? Is he upset because I got his truck dirty?* Nope, as it turns out, the problem is that I was the center of attention today. He has had enough.

And, as it turns out, so have I.

In the shower, I let the hot water run down my back while I silently cry. Every muscle in my body aches, including my heart. I realize that, even though I am in this relationship, I am alone. I am being expected to give up too much. First, it was school. Now Mr. Personality wants to take away my joy in finishing a triathlon. I deserve more than this. I am killing myself trying to make this work.

And that is when I realize I just made my decision. This marriage is over. I need to let go of my embarrassment, my shame. I allowed myself to be seduced by a rebound relationship that held out the promise of being part of a loving family – something I had been seeking for fifty years. I am too old for this foolishness and too young to settle for a broken relationship. Tomorrow, I will make my plans to move out. *On my own, again.*

MY JOURNEY TOWARD LIFE'S PURPOSE

How dense was I? I allowed myself to believe in a relationship and trusted that I would be in a safe place. Once again, promises were made, and promises were broken. I isolated myself from everyone, which eliminated any need for explanations. My son was sad but wonderfully supportive. However, he did ask me a question—a profound question—for which I had no answer: "What is it that you want, Mother?"

I have mastered the art of moving, becoming an expert in packing up my stuff, and relocating. I am beyond embarrassed and filled with shame. Once again, depression sets in. I can't see the light at the end of this overwhelming tunnel. Feeling lost has become my state of mind, my most familiar emotion. I begin journaling and schedule an appointment with my therapist. I know that I need mental and emotional support to get through this. I wish I could redo my life. I used to think that I was intelligent, independent, and self-reliant. *How could I end up with so many failed marriages? How is it that I need to keep explaining my dreams and begging for a chance to achieve them? And what the heck am I going to do now?*

Despite the turmoil of this most recent relationship disaster, I have to focus on finding a job to get me out of my financial predicament. Once again, I am not a financial winner in this upcoming divorce. Mr. Personality continues to prove that he is selfish and miserly. Thankfully, some of my old friends in medical sales tell me about a job opening. It is work that I could almost do in my sleep. With hard work and commitment, I will be able to get out of debt. In no time at all, I secure another sales position, am back on the road, traveling and working in area hospitals. Overnight stays, airports, and national conferences have become my way of life, and I am grateful. The focus on my work helps alleviate my depression. When my colleagues share stories about their wonderful spouses and relationships, I smile and listen—but I do not share. I fall back on my Academy Award-winning acting skills. No one ever figures out what is going on behind my smile.

The next few years go by quickly. I am finding joy and comfort in spending time in my new home, quietly contemplating my life with no memories of old relationships intruding into my space. I realize that, although filled with gratitude that I have a fantastic job, I am restless. I wonder.. *is this it? Is this all there is?*

I revisit my dream of becoming a medical practitioner, and partner with people who want to focus on and improve their health. I want to expand my knowledge of health care. So, I begin exploring programs. I love learning and miss being in the classroom. In no time at all, I find a graduate program, at my beloved university, in sociology focused on the impact of chronic illness on the adult population. I can utilize the information from my herbal medicine degree and the wisdom of traditional medicine in my study of contemporary challenges and research. It will provide me a unique ability to be exposed to both Eastern and Western traditions of health, wellness, and medicine. I do not have to convince anyone, explain to anyone, or make a case for myself. To be able to make a plan without having to justify it is pretty liberating. Without hesitation, I apply. And I am accepted!

I feel like a kid again, back in school! I am not the scared young woman I was years ago. This time, I know I belong here. It feels like home, and I can't wait to get started. I head toward the classroom, the building just off to my left. I am pulling open the large glass door, smiling as I remember that big wooden door many years ago. Then, I was worried about making a quick, quiet, and unassuming entrance. Now, I walk confidently inside. I am a freshman again … a freshman at fifty-something who is ready to achieve her next goal.

From the start, classes are interesting, challenging, and thought-provoking. I am doing well, holding my own. And then, it is time to take statistics. Not my area of expertise for sure. I do my best to focus. It feels like I am learning another language with complex math formulas instead of words. I have learned by now that it is best to be proactive. I immediately sign up for tutoring so that I won't fall behind. But even with help, my test results are subpar, and I decided that my next step is to speak with my professor.

Although strict in class, she is very understanding during our one-on-one. "Statistics is difficult for most students. It is a challenging course, and I know you are struggling. I have some ideas that may support your learning." She suggests a study guide and gives me handouts that allow for additional practice on assigned topics each week. "I can see in class that you are committed, and I always want your type of student to succeed. I have some limited office hours for personal tutoring if you are interested." *Interested? You bet I am!*

We meet in her office for thirty minutes every other week. She gives me extra assignments and handouts to complete that help me focus on areas where I am weak. The added work, along with our discussions, makes a significant difference in my comprehension in class and on homework assignments. I will always be grateful to her for taking the time to mentor me. I pass the course. Just barely, but I pass! It is a lesson that I will embody, help those who seek help. If you can lend a hand, do it. *Now, onward I go!*

※

The semesters fly by, and I am doing well. I will spend my final year working on an analytical paper, paired with a faculty advisor responsible for ensuring that my work meets all criteria for program completion and graduation. A second reader also reviews this paper, another faculty member who gives feedback and suggests revisions before final approval. I am thrilled to be assigned to my favorite professor, Dr. Remington, and am so pleased that he is now my primary advisor. Dr. Remington is brilliant, engaging, demanding, and yet kind. He has lectured and written extensively on the history of hospitals and Medicare in the United States, certainly an area of interest for me as well.

I tell him I want to research and write about the impact of polypharmacy on aging adults in this country. Too many adults are prescribed multiple medications, which can have a negative effect on their health and result in hospitalizations. This, in turn, puts significant burdens on our healthcare system. Dr. Remington approves my title. He finds it interesting that I will provide insight from both a personal and a systemic perspective.

I dive into researching my chosen topic. Finding data is more complicated than I imagined, especially the numbers of deaths related to the use of prescription medications. The CDC (Centers for Disease Control and Prevention) does not widely publish that statistic in the same way it publishes death by disease. There are many reasons for this, some practical and some political. In any case, the number of adults taking increasing numbers of prescription medications is growing exponentially.

The information I am uncovering makes me think of my mother. I realize that she isn't unique; she is not the only one taking at least ten medications daily. I tear through the journals and write feverishly. My previous papers on traditional and herbal medicine provide another lens with which to view the data. Each time I turn in my drafts, there are many revisions required. My pages are covered in suggested edits, marked in red. Some of the changes are expected, others are not so at all! The last suggested revision was the deletion of two sections of the paper and the addition of three paragraphs. As much as I love the work, I feel like saying, *"Are you kidding me?"* But I take a deep breath and do as instructed. In the end, these changes were genuinely going to make my paper better.

It is time to finalize my draft so that we can send a copy to our second reader. "Now, do not get too disappointed with feedback that says you have to make more changes to your paper." Dr. Remington is giving me a pep talk. "A second reader offers another perspective and their own vision for what is required to support your paper's topic." *Good grief. I am really beginning to dislike the red font on my paper!* So, off the paper goes, and I wait. And wait. Finally, I get an email to meet with Dr. Remington. My paper has been returned.

My mouth is dry as I walk into his office and slowly sit in my usual chair. His face isn't giving anything away. *Is it that bad? Is he trying to cushion the blow?* I am already on the defensive, sitting on the edge of my seat, ready to argue for my work—and he hasn't even spoken!

"Well, I must say I am pleased," he says, flipping through the paper. "There are a few minor suggestions that I concur with. I think it will be easy for you to do. Overall, I am confident that you can complete the changes in two weeks and turn your paper in for your final grade." *Really? You mean that this is a good paper, that my hard work has paid off! How fantastic!*

I race home and immediately get to work. It turns out that Dr. Remington's idea of 'minor changes' requires more work than I initially thought—more research journals and statistical analysis to support the paper's narrative. It was also suggested that I create at least two data charts to illustrate the analytics. It turns out that requires more work as well. Making the charts isn't as easy to do as I thought. But no matter. I complete the paper and drop it in the assigned mailbox. Dr. Remington and the second reader will read it a final time, my grade based on their combined feedback.

Driving home, I feel as if a huge weight has been lifted off of my shoulders. I feel lighter. No more homework. No more assignments. But what's next for me? For the past two years, I've focused only on school. It has provided a great distraction, but now I seriously need to think about what I want next. The question my son asked me two years ago, when I told him I was divorcing Mr. Personality, is still haunting me. *"What do you want, Mother?"* What, indeed?

I stop on my way home; I treat myself to a beautiful bouquet of flowers and a decadent bar of chocolate. Sitting alone at my kitchen table, I begin to journal. *Stay in gratitude, stay in creativity, stay in possibility ... What do I want my life to look like going forward?*

෫෧

The final grade for my paper is ready. My professor emails me to say that he will be in his office this afternoon if I would like to pick it up, or he will put it in the mail. I respond immediately. I will meet him at 1 o'clock. I am feeling a bit sad that my time as a student is ending. But, walking into his office, I can't stop smiling. "I just wanted to thank you so much for your support and guidance while I worked on this paper. It is a topic close to my heart, and I appreciate your insights." Hearing this, my professor smiles and sheepishly asks, "Don't you want to see your grade first?"

I open the envelope with shaking fingers. I am ecstatic about my grade! "I must tell you," my wonderful mentor says, "the biggest compliment I can give you is that our second reader said that they learned something new reading your paper and likes your style and perspective. We both hope you continue to write on this topic. It is worthy of more exploration. Continue exploring; you clearly have a passion for this material."

I don't know what to say. I just look up and smile. We chat for a few more moments, and then I leave my favorite professor's office for the last time, paper in hand. Soon, I will be walking across a stage, my newly acquired diploma in hand.

The graduation ceremony, this time, is much smaller. This particular commencement ceremony will celebrate those receiving master's degrees only. Walking through the courtyard, toward the event center entrance, there are sights and sounds of families celebrating graduates. Hugs, photos, balloons, and flowers are everywhere. The atmosphere is joyous and festive. It is not that for me. Jim is unable to make the ceremony due to a work obligation that simply could not be changed. My sisters are both living out of state and unable to make the trip. My interpretation of the declined invitations from my friends and family feel like this is my second graduate degree, so why celebrate?

As always, on the outside, my smile is beaming, and I make a point to congratulate the friends I have made in the program. I am smiling on the outside and hollow on the inside. Vanessa, my most supportive friend, took that day off to attend commencement with me today. My sadness was masked by gratitude that she made an effort. I make up my mind that I will enjoy this lovely day of ceremony, accomplishment, and appreciation.

After the ceremony, we go out to eat a celebratory lunch. Vanessa and I talk through the days' events, and I am pleased that she hasn't any inkling of my internal sadness. After all, she took the time to be here. "I have to say that I am a bit surprised that Jim couldn't make it." Vanessa looks at me curiously, "I mean, this is a big deal. Couldn't he take some vacation time?" The moment of truth for me. Do I share, or do I just pretend all is well? I only have a split second to decide; otherwise, it will look like I am stalling. After taking a quick sip of my yummy lavender lemonade, I make a decision. "Yes, I am really disappointed about it. He just did not have the ability to move an important meeting this morning. To be here this morning, he would have needed to take the train in from New York last night. The trains have been full, I am assuming due to this time of year; the season of weddings, graduations, and vacations. I know he would have been here if he could. He did call the first thing this morning, congratulating me and wished me luck." I am pleased with myself, answering without hesitation or any sign of my utter disappointment—a*ctress, always the award-winning actress.*

The truth was that Jim and I had hit a rocky patch. Similar to the time before his leaving for college. I manage to say the wrong thing and am told that I just don't 'understand him.' He is now living a fast-paced, burn-out-young lifestyle with his new New York City friends. Work is just a means to spend money on the weekend, without thinking about his future. He thinks I am a nag, and I think he is childish, much too immature for his age. The periods between our conversations are becoming longer and longer. Before this morning, we hadn't talked in a few weeks. I do my best to tell myself it is a phase that he will come around. I spend time, introspectively, trying to discover what I have done, or do, to cause this palpable friction. It is causing me great sadness and despair. I deliberately choose not to share with anyone because I feel like a maternal failure. So many of my mistakes have impacted his life; I see that clearly now.

Ironically, it brings up my own feelings of discontent with my mother. I wanted to have a relationship with her, an honest one. I wanted her to know me and support my dreams. She did not or could not do that. With my son, I make every effort to have an honest relationship with him. I support him and all of his dreams. I make it a point to verbally acknowledge when I am proud of him, supporting his accomplishments. At times, it is necessary to give my opinion based on my life experience. He has no hesitation in telling me what my faults are or how I often disappoint him. Paradoxically, I don't have the same privileges. Lately, any opinion I express is taken as a slight or an insult. If I say it is a beautiful sunny day, he would beg to differ, if only because I said it. He is a grown man in his early thirties. I know (in my brain) that I don't have the right to tell him what to do. In my heart, I just see that he is making some decisions that could lead to some big mistakes.

No matter how wonderful my friends are, I am not sharing my heartbreak with them. In many ways, I feel like this rift with my son is temporary, and I don't want to put energy into focusing on my relationship with him being fractured right now. I hold out hope that we can shift this tension and have a solid, positive relationship. Until then, I will remain silent.

I turn my focus back on Vanessa and finish up lunch. We both agree to meet up next week while walking to our cars. Driving home, I have an overwhelming feeling of isolation, of feeling entirely alone. It feels like a blanket of sadness covering me completely. I begin taking off my graduation robe before I walk in the door, immediately start folding it up and tucking it away in the closet. I grab a cup of tea, jump in the shower, and go to bed. I really wanted to stay in celebration, in gratitude, in accomplishment…and now all I want to do is go to bed. After some sleep, tomorrow will be another day. The day after my graduation, back to the routine of life.

CALLING FOR A DOCTOR

I decide, after much thought and research, to start my private practice. My foundational academic knowledge of traditional herbal medicine, nutrition practice, along with my newly acquired knowledge of current health challenges from my sociological studies, allows me to visualize what I want to do moving forward. In no time, I create my plan for my new company, take care of the legal details to register my business name, and begin designing all marketing materials. Luckily, another practitioner I know is renting office space in the area. Her practice is not busy yet, and she offers me the opportunity to sublet her office for one-half day a week. I will pay her for my rental time, making it financially advantageous for both of us. It is a beautiful and affordable space for me to build my business. *This is it! I am on my way!*

Financially, I must keep my job, continue working in sales. My practice does not provide enough income for me to eliminate outside employment at this time. I am beginning to realize that I will need to decide my future. My sales job requires long hours that extend to nights and weekends, making it difficult to progress in my practice. Changing my career path and shifting to an office position, I will have the freedom to build up my clientele by working a standard workweek, with holidays, nights, and weekends off.

It is a big step; just thinking about it causes my stomach to be in knots. No matter what, I know I have to decide how I want to move forward. What is my vision? What am I called to do? Just as I have always done in the past, I continue to push myself, somehow pushing through fear toward my goal. This is no different. I just need to do my homework, make my plan, envision success, be willing to do the work, and move forward. *Onward I go…again!*

After many months of applications and interviews, I finally receive an offer for a position as an office coordinator supporting community health outreach programs. This position offers a set, weekly schedule; only forty hours per week. No travel to conferences, no hospital overnight training sessions, and it is close to my house. The pay, however, is significantly less. This decision is becoming agonizing. I can see this office position would be in line with my desire to stay in health and wellness. The hours afford the ability to deliver community outreach programs for them during my eight-hour day and allow me to build my business on my own time, simultaneously. Deep down, I know this is a great opportunity and want to accept it. I am just not sure I can make the "money work." Money is a genuine concern and source of worry for me. No financial safety net, my savings account a casualty of my divorces. Building my business will require money I don't have right now.

Additionally, I need income to cover my monthly living expenses. It is undoubtedly going to have to be a 'leap of faith.' *Do I have the nerve?*

After a tense few days of contemplation, budget-making plans, sleepless nights, and journaling, I finally make my decision. As always, I "insert confidence here" and accept the office position. I thought I would feel immediate relief once I made my decision. I do not. I continue to second guess my decision wondering if I have made a mistake and haven't even started yet! My fears and concerns slowly subside as I focus on being successful in my new office job. The people I work with are wonderfully talented, welcoming, and genuinely compassionate coworkers. After work, it is now routine to spend many evening hours in my home office to build up my new business. I view it as having a second job; for all practical purposes, it truly is.

I have created several workshops focusing on health that I deliver to the community at various community centers. *I am in heaven!* The audience response has been overwhelmingly positive, and having the opportunity to meet and speak with women about their health and wellness is invigorating. With practice, I am honing my message, my view and concept of **Nourishment**. I dig into the research and incorporate evidence-based recommendations in my presentations. Creating visually appealing and interactive lectures has required me to tap into my creativity, leading me to deliver more powerfully. I also decide to add a few cooking demos, and they are a hit as well.

My small practice is slowly building, with a steady group of clients. I love being able to work with women seeking guidance on health goals. Supporting them with recommendations on food choices, herbal support, and lifestyle shifts is most rewarding. And….I am feeling the need to explore ways to enhance my skills. I realize that I am yearning to increase my academic knowledge and clinical skills that would enable me to improve as a practitioner. Hmmm….

It's a lazy Sunday morning in April, the warm sun shining brightly into the living room. As I pour my second cup of lavender chamomile tea, the phone rings. Jim is calling to check-in. "Well, hello stranger! This is a nice surprise!" I decide it is best to sound bubbly instead of perturbed that it has been months since we last spoke. It is a pleasant conversation, and it feels good to catch up on all of his news. I share my thoughts about potentially exploring the possibility of looking at doctoral-level academic programs. I wait, conditioned to expect a negative response to my goal of attending school. "Mother," he says, as I take a deep breath, "it is no surprise at all that you are looking to go back to school. You love school, and I think it's great." I am stunned, pleasantly stunned.

"Wow, I can't tell you how wonderful it is to hear that!" We talk through a couple of ideas, and he suggests a few programs for me to consider. "Look at doctoral programs in public health or aging studies that may be a perfect fit for you. I can only imagine how challenging a Ph.D. program is. Better you than me!" We laugh and shift the subject. He asks me to take a few days off to visit him in New York. He did not have to ask twice; mentally I have already booked my train ticket. I love the city and enjoy spending time with my son, especially when we get along well.

My notepad is filling up with academic program options, requirements, deadlines, and tuition fee schedules. My head is swimming with details. Nothing feels right, not finding that "perfect fit" the way I have done in the past. I put everything away and decide I will revisit this later. My days, nights, and weekends are spent working my two jobs, researching journal articles, and creating nourishment recommendation plans for my clients.

I look forward to getting on the train tomorrow morning to see Jim. I am thrilled to be spending time with him, enjoying our trips to museums, walking in Central Park, and eating at his favorite restaurants. It is turning out to be a spectacular trip! Our conversations range from the silly to the substantive. We delve into the root causes of some of our disagreements. The reasons why we butt heads at times. I jokingly tell him that he inherited my stubborn, focused, intense genes while also inheriting his dad's creative, artistic, and laid-back genes. He certainly inherited his dad's view on money. It makes me crazy—no planning for the future or being mindful to live within your means. I simply don't understand the 'live fast, die young' mentality. We agree to disagree and move on. Even this discussion ends on a positive note, with no tension at all.

On the train ride home, I begin to daydream as I watch the scenery whizzing by in the window. The sun warms my face as I watch my progress from New York through Pennsylvania on my way home to Maryland. I am completely relaxed listening to the music on my iPod. Suddenly it comes to me! I remember reading something about a doctoral program in nutrition at the same university I attended for herbal medicine. Of course! Why didn't I look into this sooner? I quickly dig out my cell phone out of my purse. *No time like the present to get started!*

I barely get inside my houser, throw my bag on my bed, and head up to my home office. Booting up my computer, I begin to print information related to the Doctor of Clinical Nutrition program. My printer is churning out paper for quite some time. I sink into my seat and begin reading with purpose. My excitement intensifies when I read the description of the program and the requirements for admission. I can see that I am a perfect match for this program! Yes!!

I immediately begin drafting my plans to see if I can make this work, both from a time commitment and financial perspective. I can't contain my excitement any longer, and the decision is made. I am going to apply to this program. Without hesitation, I begin working on my application.

Here I go…again!

My acceptance message arrives. I have been accepted into the doctoral program! Classes begin in September. Back in the classroom, such joy and excitement!

I am part of a diverse, brilliantly talented, and successful group of students. The work is grueling and intensive. I remind myself that it will all be worth it as the sleepless nights pile up. Living alone, I no longer hide my books. I no longer have to take care of anyone but myself.

At times, it feels like I have been in this program for over one hundred years; other times, time goes by quickly. One trimester blends into the next, with a constant stream of assignments, papers, discussion threads, and research topics. Nights and weekends are spent at my computer, either creating or editing drafts to be turned in. Life has taken on a familiar cadence.

Thankfully, I am quickly approaching the end of the trimester and our upcoming holiday break. Jim will be visiting for Christmas this year, so I am excited to turn in the final assignments. My last paper is turned in, and I sit down in my living room feeling an incredible sense of accomplishment. One more year to go, and I will have completed my doctorate. I look around and begin to mentally make plans to decorate for the holidays and Jim's arrival.

When he walks in the door, I am stunned. Jim looks horrible, gaunt-pale, and rail-thin. He doesn't appear to notice my surprise. He walks in and greets me with a flat tone of voice. "Are you okay? You look a little pale," is all I can manage to say.

"Yes, I am just exhausted. Been working long hours, and the train was crammed full." He sits down on the sofa and turns on the television. We exchange superficial pleasantries before dinner. I tell myself that I am over-reacting, and he is just tired. He will feel better tomorrow. One of his favorite activities is, and always has been, decorating for Christmas.

After dinner, he helps clean up and says he is going to get to bed early. I stay up a bit, unable to sleep, with a nagging sense of dread making it impossible to think about sleep.

The following day is more of the same. Jim looks frail and sickly, looking like he has a terrible case of the flu. Again, I ask if he is feeling alright. As I hand him a cup of herbal tea, he asks me to sit down. He wants to talk. My heart stops, my mind is racing. I just know, instinctually, there is terrible news heading my way. It turns out my instincts are spot on.

My son's life in the fast lane has caught up with him in a profound way. He is spinning out of control, and now recognizes he needs help. I want to run out of the room, I want to scream, I want to pretend this is a dream. I listen to him and do my very best not to react. This is not the time to argue. This is the time for me to feel compassion and provide solace to my son. After he shares his story, we sit in silence. I jump up and give him a big hug and tell him we will figure this out—both terrified of what lies ahead. Neither of us knows the next steps yet.

As always, I put my emotions aside and spring into action. "We need to find a place for you to go to get help." Even as I say it, I don't know what it means. We find suitable places and begin making phone calls. Availability is an issue, as are finances. Insurance is not an option. All expenses for care will be out of pocket. "Money is money. Your health is most important," I say as we find a highly recommended facility. They have space for him, and we make the arrangements. He will leave tomorrow. There is no time to ponder, his life depends on him getting a bed in this facility.

My holidays have gone from celebratory to being consumed by my complete and utter despair. My home feels empty. Jim left this morning on his way to begin to rebuild his life. I am too numb to cry. It takes a few days before I grasp what just happened.

The clock strikes midnight, signaling the start of the new year. My last year in the doctoral program. This was supposed to be a celebratory night. Jim and I were planning to have a lovely, relaxing holiday and festive new year. How did this happen? What did I miss? The guilt is overwhelming, the sense of failure palpable. I am not sure how much more I can take. The abyss is calling me…again. The darkness is taking over, and I am absolutely terrified I will be swallowed up in it. I genuinely have no vision of how to get through this.

"Here we are, our last year of the program. I trust that you all had a lovely break, were able to rest, and enjoy time with your families." Our professor goes on to detail the next trimester's expectations. "Enjoy this time as you continue through your program. It will be challenging and most rewarding. Graduation is in sight!" With that, the class begins to clap, and collectively we all cheer. Break time is filled with stories of holiday trip details, gifts received, and discussion of upcoming graduation plans.

I cleverly make my way out of the room, as I no longer have enough energy for another acting performance. No one notices that I have left, so there is no need to explain. I will keep this news to myself. Somehow I will get through. I will have to compartmentalize. Stay focused on tasks at hand, and fall apart later. Our weekend class intensive is soon over, and I am heading home. There is an emptiness in my heart, an utter feeling of complete depression. I fall into bed, without having enough energy to even change my clothes.

These last months have been intense. I am smiling during the day, participating in class, and falling apart at night. Jim is doing much better, making incredible strides toward his future. I will get the chance to visit him in a few weeks. Taking time away from classes requires me to "work ahead" to ensure all assignments are turned in before due dates, and I need to contact my professors for approval. This is a crossroads for me. Do I share the reason why? Or just give them a generic 'family emergency' excuse? With all the energy I can muster, I email my professor. She responds immediately, and we set up a time to speak.

I begin slowly by saying that I need to take a week away and make arrangements to get my assignments in before leaving. Although I did my best, my voice cracked and 'gave me away.' My acting skills, it seems, are on the blink. Before I know it, I am sharing 'the truth.' My son is in an in-patient facility, getting treatment, and needs my attention. The words are pouring out. I can't stop them. Tears follow.

We make plans for my assignments, and my professor suggests that I send an email to my other instructors with the same request. "Share what you feel comfortable with, and allow us to support you at this time," she tells me as I slowly compose myself. I want this to be a nightmare from which I will soon awaken. It is not. It is reality, my reality.

※

Months are passing by quickly. School has taken on a frenetic pace, as we are all stretching ourselves to get to the finish line. Jim is doing well, making significant progress toward building his new life. We talk often, and I am inspired by his grit, honesty, and willingness to take responsibility. He moved to Connecticut, which has turned out to be a blessing. He has surrounded himself with an incredibly supportive team. While I miss him terribly, I see that this is a good move for him.

We have both been through so much over these many months. Jim and I make plans to celebrate our successes, my graduation, and his "move to his new life." We both agree that May will be our big weekend. It is so lovely to be making such joyous plans…plans that celebrate happiness! I can't wait! In just two weeks, it will be March, the finish line clearly in sight.

GRADUATION AND A FINAL GOODBYE

March signifies the transition to spring, one of my favorite seasons. But March 2020 brought unexpected news ... news that I would be working remotely, quarantining, and practicing social distancing due to the COVID-19 pandemic. Joy and anticipation turned into anxiety and uncertainty. I stayed glued to daily televised briefings from our governor. I scoured social media for breaking news and made numerous phone calls to friends. No one could predict what was to come, what the impact of the pandemic would be. The virus rocked my world.

The finish line is in sight. This marathon will soon be in my rearview mirror. Just a few more assignments to turn in, and my program is complete. I can't wait to receive my confirmation letter from the registrar's office! I begin to daydream about how I will spend my free time, time without studying, writing, or prepping for exams staring me in the face.

I am smiling as I think about the endless possibilities and begin to finalize plans for family and close friends to attend my graduation activities—booking airline travel, making post-ceremony dinner reservations, and finalizing hotel rooms. Family and friends will be arriving by trains, planes, and automobiles. Everyone is excited and looking forward to the upcoming celebrations.

※

An email confirms that I have been cleared for graduation! I'm walking on air! My mind is still processing the news, and my face now has a permanent smile!

※

Unfortunately, in the blink of an eye, my entire world has changed.

Following CDC guidance, an announcement at our staff meeting details the plan for the next few weeks. Our building will close. We all shift into high gear, making arrangements for our entire staff to work from home. I pack my things for the big relocation.

I want to stay in gratitude. I am healthy. I have a job that accommodates working remotely. And, I have amazing people in my life. Despite all these positives, sadness lies right under the surface. This is not what I envisioned—not at all.

Next month, my colleagues from my doctoral program and I planned to have one last weekend together as a group, a close-knit group that just spent the previous three years together. Now no final celebratory get-together. Conversations with my family have gone from celebratory to being filled with concern and anxiety. I feel sorry for myself despite my attempts to remain positive.

Days have turned into weeks, with no end in sight. The pandemic news continues to be grim and more uncertain every day. Social distancing means the elimination of all group activities. I am reading a message I just received from the provost of the university. I re-read it to be sure I understand it correctly: ... It is necessary to cancel our commencement. I begin to cry. This can't be! This was to be an occasion where we would all be able to spend time celebrating my accomplishment. I will have to cancel all of our plans, flights, and hotel reservations. In essence, cancel all face-to-face and in-person celebrations.

I sit and quietly stare at my letter confirming that I am cleared for graduation, telling myself that this is a dream, that I will wake up. *This isn't a dream, Carla. Get on with it.* As I am canceling airline, hotel, and restaurant reservations, I remind myself how much I have to be thankful for. But that doesn't stop my tears.

April slowly shifts into May. Unceremoniously, I receive an email message that I am now Dr. Carla Johnston. Via Zoom calls, I share the news with my son, sisters, and friends. "Commencement will take place virtually this year. It won't be live so you can view the ceremony at your leisure." Sitting at a computer just isn't the same as celebrating in person. Seeing tiles of family and friends on the screen is lackluster, compared to sharing hugs, laughter, and celebratory toasts over glasses of wine and sparkling cider.

It is Friday afternoon when my cell phone rings. The caller says she is a nurse in the hospital intensive care unit. My mother was just admitted. "She had a nasty fall requiring immediate medical attention, and her condition is rapidly deteriorating." The kindness in the nurse's voice is little comfort as she says, "I am sorry to say that she is not doing well, and we need to speak to the family member in charge of your mother's medical wishes. Does she have a DNR, a Do Not Resuscitate order? She is unable to speak, and she is quite agitated. She doesn't appear to be able to comprehend what we're telling her."

In shock at what I am hearing, I slowly sink into my chair. I have not talked to my mother in more than ten years. Our relationship was always tricky, and we'd gone for long periods in the past without speaking to each other. We never figured each other out, never found that common mother-daughter ground. Occasionally, I would reach out, but she wasn't ready. Ironically, I am confident my mother would say the same thing about me.

It takes a minute to comprehend everything the nurse is telling me and what I need to do, but I assure the nurse that I will get back to her within the hour.

Shifting into high gear, I quickly call Ann and Louise and explain the situation. Thankfully, we are on the same page regarding what our mother envisioned for end-of-life interventions. I call the hospital and relay that my mother wouldn't want a DNR, and then ask about the next steps.

After a pause, the nurse says, "Because of the pandemic, there's a mandated no-visitor policy in place. But we made arrangements yesterday for another patient to have a family member make a brief visit, and we can offer that option to you. To move forward, you would need to confirm that you can quarantine for fourteen days after the visit." I am the only logical choice to be the visitor, the only daughter living within driving distance who can quarantine after the visit. My head is spinning—no time to think. *Just get on the phone and make the necessary plans.*

The two-hour drive to the hospital gives me time to think about what I want to say to my mother after all these years. I can't recall ever packing so quickly, and I am not sure I have what I will need. As the miles and minutes pass, I begin to rehearse out loud what I will say.

Security at the hospital is expecting me. I fill out a raft of forms, have my temperature taken, and am escorted to the ICU. The nurse greets me, and we walk to my mother's room. I have spent my career walking hospital hallways. But now it is personal. My mother is here, gravely ill. I can't breathe and begin to feel as if I will pass out. Will she recognize me? Be glad to see me? Or will she be upset that I am here? How will I get through this?

I take a deep breath and enter my mother's room. She looks so frail and small in the hospital bed. The nurse touches my mother's shoulder and bends close to her ear, telling her that I am here. My mother slowly turns her head to look at me and makes an effort to smile. She tries to speak, but only grunts and groans escape. She is visibly frustrated and uses every bit of her strength to gesture with her eyes. "Yes, I see that you are trying to talk." the nurse calmly says, "Your daughter is here now. She is here to be with you."

I am on autopilot, reflexively leaning on many years of practice working in hospitals as I put on disposable gloves and sit down next to her. "Hi Mom, I am happy to see you." All my rehearsing in the car was for nothing. I am lost, with no idea what to say. But stuttering, I press on, "The hospital won't allow anyone else to visit. I have my cell phone, and we can call everyone ... is that okay with you?" She blinks.

Is that a yes or a no? Is she just too tired or upset that I am here? I feel helpless. Not knowing if it's right, I begin dialing. I spent the next few hours holding the phone next to my mother's ear. Briefly but noticeably, she smiles as she hears each new voice. My nieces and nephews opt to video chat, and they are as pleased to see her as she is to see them.

The nurse comes back into the room, asking if I could join her at the desk. "Your mother is terminal, and we are making arrangements for her to go into hospice. A hospice bed just opened up, so we need to move quickly." She goes on to explain that my mother will be transferred in a few hours and, as preparations are made, I call my sisters with the news. The hospice will make sure everyone in the family is updated. In a haze, I slowly make my way to the parking garage, then head for the hospice center.

The hospice staff is as lovely as the staff at the hospital was. They make every effort to help me feel comfortable as they explain the process and plans moving forward. While settling into a recliner next to my mother's bed, a nurse walks in and asks, "Would you like something to eat? You look exhausted, Carla." I smile, telling her that I am not hungry and thanking her for her kindness.

I need to focus, concentrate, and keep moving. In some ways, this experience is oddly familiar. When there is a crisis, I spring into action. Get through it, and then think about it later. I tell myself that I will have plenty of time to cry in the future. Not now, later ... always later. I glance at my mother and see she is sleeping. I decide to close my eyes and rest for just a few minutes.

The rising sun brings bright light into the room, immediately waking me up. My mother is very pale, and her breathing is shallow.

She doesn't open her eyes in response to a day-shift nurse introducing herself. The nurse tells me that my mother is unresponsive. "She is transitioning toward the dying process. Hearing is the last sense to go," she gently explains, "so please feel free to continue talking and reading to her."

On autopilot again, I begin to make calls, hold the phone next to my mother's ear. There are no more smiles, no signs of recognition. A few family members want to video chat to have the chance to see her while saying goodbye. I honor all their requests, doing the best I can to ensure everyone has enough time with her. My sisters and son are wonderfully supportive, asking what they can do to help me. I realize how difficult this is for them. They are not able to here in person. Instead, they have to rely on my phone as they say their goodbyes.

The evening nurse walks into the room, "I know you have not left the room or eaten anything. Here is a sandwich and a cup of tea for you." My eyes fill with tears that I am unable to hold back. During this period of crisis in dealing with COVID-19, she is taking care of my mother ... and now me. What a thoughtful gesture.

Time is running out. What do I want to say to my mother? How do I do this? My mouth is dry, and my voice is shaking. "Mother, I am here," I begin. "Do you feel my hand?" No response. "You are not alone; we are all here for you."

I take a deep breath and continue, "I hope you can hear me. I want to say that I am sorry for any pain I caused you. I am asking you to forgive me for being a difficult daughter at times. I also want you to know that I forgive you for being a difficult mother at times. I think that we both did the best we could. We are all here, your daughters, grandchildren, friends. We are all here." I look for any sign, any movement to signal that she hears me. There are none.

A priest enters the room. Honoring Ann's request, I call her and place my phone on the bed so she can hear the priest administer last rites to our mother. My brain is numb. I am not sure how much more I can process. I sit back in the recliner and, closing my eyes, listen to my sister cry faintly in the background.

Some time quietly passes, and I begin talking again, filling this silence with a conversation, sharing details about my most recent academic accomplishment with my mother. At age fifty-eight, I am still hoping to hear my mother say she is proud of me. I fall silent, feeling childish and silly. Still, who could have guessed that I would be spending my graduation weekend in a hospice?

A knock at the door breaks the silence, and a nurse enters the room. Shift change, already? I notice someone walking in behind her. I tilt my head and instinctually smile. Is that …. is that…Jim? Am I losing my mind? I just spoke with him when he called to check on me. The nurse is smiling broadly. "We have a surprise for you … your son has arrived!" Surprise? My son has arrived?

I jump up and give Jim a big hug as he tells me the story. "We have been working over these past few hours to make arrangements for me to be here. The nurses worked hard to get special permission, to allow two of us to be in this room." I can't contain my emotions. I have always been the one taking care of others, making plans, getting things done. I am no longer alone. My son, Jim, is here with me.

He has a confidence about him, a strength that I hadn't noticed before. In no time, he begins to rearrange the room, making it possible for us to talk to each other and my mother—even taking the initiative to have a small lamp brought in and turning off the annoying overhead light. A nice difference! Job well done. We both smile and settle in for the next few hours.

The room is still; everything is quiet. The night is creeping by. Suddenly, Jim sits up in his chair. I notice it as well. My mother's breathing is now barely audible. It is time for us to say our final goodbyes. We take her hands and tell her how much we love her. There are no gasps, no sounds at all. At 2:51 am, she slowly exhales. Then ... silence. She's gone.

My son slowly leaves the room, giving me time to gather my thoughts, take in this final moment, and begin processing the last few days. After a few quiet minutes, BOOM ... we begin the "business" of death. Papers need signatures, funeral directors need direction, and belongings need to be packed up. We have gone from silence to harried activity. And now, time to leave.

My son and I walk the now-familiar hallway one last time, making our way to the parking lot. Walking in companionable silence, I notice that we share the same cadence. We hug at our cars—no need to speak. We silently smile at each other and drive away.

LIFE'S LESSONS LEARNED

Upon reflection, I realize just how much of my life I spent explaining my vision and desires. I surrounded myself with those who found value in my ability to completely support them, to be their enthusiastic cheerleader. And I never expected the same in return. I made it easy for others to put themselves first and me second; I set up my relationships that way. I now recognize that, for most of my life, I was asking for permission. Needlessly. I deserve to be supported and celebrated.

I am also keenly aware that most of us have challenges that we do not share easily. I have spent many years designing—and hiding behind—a beautiful facade for all the world to see. I keep that realization in the front of my mind when I work with my clients and patients. What they choose to share with me about their health may just be the tip of their iceberg. I respect that. I hold compassion and empathy for them.

Sharing our deepest pain, disappointments, embarrassment, and shame requires strength and trust. When we are sick and in poor health, diving into those emotions can feel overwhelming. I feel as if my life has given me the ability to sit with someone experiencing pain, isolation, fear, or anxiety; I know what each of those emotions feels like. Even if I do not share my personal experiences, I can tap into them to be present for those I am helping.

We all have our own challenges and experiences, our own unique story. It is the judgment we feel from others that creates separation and causes us to shut down. I continue to work on my shame and the embarrassment I hold from so many failed relationships. I still worry that I will be judged as a failure. By contrast, I find myself judging others less. I tend to "look beyond the headlines" with individuals and wonder what led to their upsets. I am less concerned with pointing out failures and more focused on celebrating successes because there are always successes. Even when I feel let down now, I can still find many things to celebrate.

I tenaciously pursued a dream of being part of a loving family. I spent many years in relationships that did not, could not fulfill that dream. I stayed, thinking that I could make my dream come true. It is what I wanted for myself and my son. Now, I realize that I actually DO have, and am part of, a loving family. It is just different from what I envisioned. What I was looking for, I have, in another form. Jim and my sisters are my family. They continue to be supportive and inspire me toward my new goals and dreams. This is a big lesson, one that I will continue to pay attention to as I get older. It is the basis for my gratitude.

Being a mom at such a young age was not easy. I certainly made my fair share of mistakes. It has always been important to me that Jim felt loved, supported, and able to step out in the world and create his own vision. I am thrilled that we have a fantastic relationship, one based on honesty. Jim has inherited his father's creative spirit and talent and with my stubbornness and tenacity, the best of both of us. I could not be more proud of him, his accomplishments, and his ability to maintain focus on his goals. Our conversations about life are substantive and thought-provoking. It wasn't always easy; he and I butted heads over the years. And in retrospect, I know that was part of our mother/child journey. Sadly, my mother and I never shared that journey. We could never get beyond our mistakes to move our relationship forward.

Even becoming a college graduate wasn't what I thought it would be. I smile now when I think about the stereotypical image of a freshman starting college. In my mind's eye, I see a young person leaving home and making their way in the world, having to create a life of their own and explore their path toward adulthood.

Interestingly, that is what happened to me. It just did not happen upon graduating high school. To those who tell me, "You are so lucky, you got your degree." I want to say: luck really had little to do with it. Preparation, tenacity, grit, dedication, and sacrifice did. It is natural to watch those crossing the finish line or walking across the stage and forget about the drive, the hours of focus it took to get there. Now, when I hear of an accomplishment, I make sure to note the enormous achievement of sticking with it and doing what was required to succeed. I now use the term 'freshman' to describe new learning about to take place; a freshman is a beginner who aspires to learn more. My goal is to always be a freshman at something—because I am always excited about learning new things. I left the home I had and began discovering and exploring who I wanted to be. Getting out there on my own, depending upon myself to make decisions and creating my own path. I did that, and I am continuing to do that.

"What is next?" It is a question I am often asked. "Now that you finally earned your doctorate, what's next?" There is no simple answer. The exploration continues. It has never been about simply getting my degree. It has always been about being a knowledgeable and compassionate practitioner. By earning degrees in traditional medicine, supplemented with other degrees focused on contemporary medicine, and clinical nutrition practice, I am able to offer a unique perspective on health and wellness.

I enjoy the privilege of working with women who want to focus on their health. Some are challenged with life-altering diagnoses. Others want to continue on their wellness journey. I am committed to cultivating conversations with women about their health and wellness goals. This means expanding our focus beyond nutrition to include those things in our lives that support overall wellness; namely my vision of Nourishment. My doctorate in clinical nutrition, from a functional medicine and integrative health perspective, puts it all together in a dynamic way. I am passionate about creating programs that will allow women to find their unique path to a life of nourishment, strength, and peace.

I love learning. That won't change. Maybe I will learn how to open my heart to a supportive relationship. Perhaps I will teach other women to pursue their dreams, no matter their age. As I approach my sixth decade, I have developed a second wind to pursue new dreams and goals.

So, what is next? I don't know for sure. I do know, whatever it is, it will be exciting!

ABOUT THE AUTHOR

Carla Johnston, DCN, MA, MS, CNS, LDN

Dr. Carla Johnston holds a Doctorate in Clinical Nutrition from the Maryland University of Integrative Health, an M.S. in Herbal Medicine from the University of Integrative Health, and an M.A. in Applied Sociology University of Maryland, Baltimore County. She is a board-certified Clinical Nutrition Specialist through the American Nutrition Association and a licensed nutritionist in Maryland.

Carla has more than 25 years' experience in healthcare as an account manager responsible for sales, clinical support, and education for products used in operating suites and intensive care units within area hospitals. At mid-life, she shifted her career trajectory, exploring programs steeped in mind-body medicine traditions. Through the pursuit of academic programs focused on these principles, she started her clinical practice specializing in providing nutrition education for women aged fifty and older; creating her signature Nourishment programs, workshops, and courses.

www.ingramcontent.com/pod-product-compliance
Lightning Source LLC
Chambersburg PA
CBHW050324120526
44592CB00014B/2046